C0-AEM-665

THE PRACTICE OF NEWSPAPER MANAGEMENT

W. Parkman Rankin

PRAEGER SPECIAL STUDIES • PRAEGER SCIENTIFIC

New York • Philadelphia • Eastbourne, UK
Toronto • Hong Kong • Tokyo • Sydney

Library of Congress Cataloging-in-Publication Data

Rankin, William Parkman
    The practice of newspaper management.

    Includes index.
    1. Newspaper publishing. 2. Newspapers–
Circulation. I. Title.
PN4734.R36 1986   070.5'72   85-28099
ISBN 0-03-005352-8 (alk. paper)

Published in 1986 by Praeger Publishers
CBS Educational and Professional Publishing, a Division of CBS Inc.
521 Fifth Avenue, New York, NY 10175 USA

© 1986 by Praeger Publishers

All rights reserved

6789 052 987654321

Printed in the United States of America on acid-free paper

INTERNATIONAL OFFICES

Orders from outside the United States should be sent to the appropriate address listed below. Orders from areas not listed below should be placed through CBS International Publishing, 383 Madison Ave., New York, NY 10175 USA

Australia, New Zealand
Holt Saunders, Pty. Ltd., 9 Waltham St., Artarmon, N.S.W. 2064, Sydney, Australia

Canada
Holt, Rinehart & Winston of Canada, 55 Horner Ave., Toronto, Ontario, Canada M8Z 4X6

Europe, the Middle East, & Africa
Holt Saunders, Ltd., 1 St. Anne's Road, Eastbourne, East Sussex, England BN21 3UN

Japan
Holt Saunders, Ltd., Ichibancho Central Building, 22-1 Ichibancho, 3rd Floor, Chiyodaku, Tokyo, Japan

Hong Kong, Southeast Asia
Holt Saunders Asia, Ltd., 10 Fl, Intercontinental Plaza, 94 Granville Road, Tsim Sha Tsui East, Kowloon, Hong Kong

Manuscript submissions should be sent to the Editorial Director, Praeger Publishers, 521 Fifth Avenue, New York, NY 10175 USA

to Ruth

FOREWORD

If the newspaper executive, the advertising executive, the educator, or the student does not use Dr. W. Parkman Rankin's book, *The Practice of Newspaper Management*, they will be one brick short of a load in having the answers from every standpoint needed in newspaper management today. It is a book, skillfully written, that should be the mandatory handbook of executive practitioners in the fascinating world of newspapers.

Dr. Rankin, known to me as Perk, for many, many years, has been a friend, confidante, and advisor to all of us in this wonderfully changing business. Perhaps he should be referred to as "The Dean" in view of his long stretch in time and breadth of knowledge of what goes on in newspapers. He ought to know – he was there.

This book on newspapers has a layout (as they say in advertising) of twelve chapters, heavily covering the marketing aspects of newspapering, as well as the fine art of managing and planning.

You will be delighted with his run-down on America's two largest newspaper organizations, that is, the American Newspaper Publishers Association, and the Newspaper Advertising Bureau. The writer carefully leads the reader through the maze of functions in both organizations, developing full knowledge of what one needs to know to utilize the impact these influential organizations have.

You will also be fascinated with Perk's file notes on new developments in "the business" giving the reader an opportunity to rub shoulders with the newspaper entrepreneurial giants who are running on the new creative fast track. You will get insider information on the futurists of the newspaper business.

In addition, fine case histories telling of America's outstanding regional newspapers are also part of the package.

I salute Perk Rankin for covering the practice of newspaper management in a fascinating way, of which only he is capable.

Edward W. Estlow
President and C.E.O.
Scripps-Howard

PREFACE

After searching for the past two years for a suitable textbook related to the business management of daily newspapers for my classes in Print Media Management, I finally came to the conclusion that I should write my own.

Hence this book, which I hope will serve as a guide to college students, undergraduate and graduate, to media executives at both the advertising agency and client levels, and to newspaper staff members and executives.

In these pages I combine my own 40 years of experience at magazines and newspapers with personal interviews with leading executives in the newspaper business. It has been my privilege and pleasure to have known all of these executives personally for many years and I shall always be grateful for their willingness to share their words of wisdom.

I am indebted to scores of persons for their many contributions to the content of this book, with special gratitude to the following: from Arizona State University: Dean Nicholas Henry, Professors El Dean Bennett, Douglas Anderson, and Richard McCafferty; from the Washington Post Company: Mrs. Katharine Graham, chairman, Donald Graham, publisher, and Guyon Knight, vice-president, corporate communications; from Scripps-Howard: Edward W. Estlow, president; from the *Los Angeles Times*: Vance Stickell, executive vice-president, and Joellen Kitchen, director of promotion and public relations; from the Dispatch Printing Company: Thomas B. Sherrill, vice-president; from the Phoenix Newspapers, Incorporated: Darrow Tully, publisher, Conrad A. Kloh, director of sales and marketing, Kenneth Clouse, advertising director, William R. Shover, community and corporate services director, Donald L. Martz, circulation director, Ellen Baar Jacobs, market research manager, Mark Geffert, advertising sales superviser, David Hume, promotion manager, and David Kampf, sales development coordinator; from the American Newspaper Publishers Association: Jerry W. Friedman, executive vice-president, and Joseph J. Lorfano, public affairs specialist; from the Newspaper Advertising Bureau: Craig C. Standen, president, Leo Bogart, executive vice-president, and Mac G. Morris, vice-president; from the Audit Bureau of Circulations: M. David Keil, president and managing director, and Charles O. Bennett, vice-president, communications; from the International Circulation Managers Association; Joseph B. Forsee, general manager; from *Editor & Publisher*: Robert U. Brown, president and editor; from International Newspaper Advertising and Marketing Executives: Sidney W. Bordelon, general manager, and Susan M. Schoebel, administrative assistant; from *The New York Times*: Elliott M. Sanger, Jr., manager, corporate relations, and Robert S. Czufin, advertising manager; from the *Chicago Tribune*: Robert M. Hunt, president, and John McCutcheon, Tribune Archives.

I am also grateful to several others whose ideas and encouragement were most helpful: Eugene S. Waggaman, Jr., associate marketing services director, *Newsweek* magazine; Ted Slate, library director of *Newsweek*; Mrs. Mary Lou Allen of the Walter Cronkite School of Journalism and Telecommunication at Arizona State University, who typed the manuscript and offered valuable suggestions along the way. My thanks also to Catherine Woods, economics editor; Alison Podel, business editor; and Susan Alkana, project editor of Praeger Special Studies for their patience and editing talent.

My warmest gratitude goes to my wife, Ruth Gerard Rankin, who offered constructive criticism and encouragement during the preparation of the book.

It is hoped that this book will not only be used as a text in leading schools of journalism and business throughout the country but will also end up on the desks of practicing newspaper people. Another desire is that the book will encourage talented young people to enter a field of business endeavor that will prove stimulating, interesting, and profitable.

Contents ———————————————

1

INTRODUCTION

> Were it left to me to decide whether we should have a
> government without newspapers, or newspapers without govern-
> ment, I should not hesitate a moment to prefer the latter.
> –Thomas Jefferson, 1787

EARLY HISTORY

Daily newspapers have become an integral part of our life. On any given weekday, more than 65.6 million newspapers will be printed and read in the United States and Canada.

More than 109 million people will read one newspaper and many will read two or more.

Seventy percent of all adults read a newspaper "yesterday." Those people who didn't read a newspaper yesterday will most likely see one before the week is over. In the last five days, 89 percent of adults 18 years and older have read a newspaper.

Newspapers function as a unique and vital force in the daily lives of millions of Americans. They provide the facts and analysis that allow informed citizens to make effective and responsible decisions, not only in coping with the complexities of modern living, but also in protecting the rights and liberties of a free society.

Each day more than 100 million people rely on newspaper professionals to provide accurate, timely, and useful information to help them plan their daily lives; to advise, instruct, educate, challenge and entertain.

By David Kampf

To fulfill their mandate in a free society, newspapers must remain strong and independent institutions, free to express their views and opinions without political or economic coercion or restraint. Economic strength and constant vigilance are vital to the maintenance of such independence.

Newspapers remain economically sound despite the challenges of new technology, changing life styles and the economic evolutions of recent years.[1]

The first newspaper published in the United States was Benjamin Harris' *Publick Occurrences Both Foreign and Domestick*. It was printed in Boston on September 25, 1690. This venture was soon suppressed by the governor of Massachusetts and his council because the "paper contained certain reflections of a very high nature and was printed without the required license."[2]

It was unfortunate that this first attempt at newspaper publishing in our country was killed because Harris had lofty ideals and promised that his newspaper's purpose would be, in part, to help people comprehend the "Circumstances of Publique Affairs," so as to assist their businesses and negotiations. Harris also planned to publish his newspaper with businesslike regularity and continuity.[3]

A man far different from Benjamin Harris succeeded in starting a newspaper in April 1704 that was "printed by authority" and continued for 15 years. His name was John Campbell, a cautious promoter who named his newspaper the *Boston News-Letter*. The eighteenth century was a time of growing maturity, complexity, and more of everything: trade, money, migrants, schools, churches, roads, and books. Such an age could support newspapers: from 1719 to 1783 no fewer than 67 publishers started newspapers, and more than 30 newspapers survived to the time of the Revolution in 1776.[4]

Other newspapers that followed included the *New England Courant*, begun in 1721 by James Franklin who employed his brother, Benjamin, in his printing shop.

The first newspaper outside Boston was Andrew Bradford's *American Weekly Mercury*, founded in Philadelphia in 1719. Andrew's father, William Bradford, started the first New York paper, the *Gazette*, in 1725. Benjamin Franklin published the *Pennsylvania Gazette* from 1729 to 1766. The first daily newspaper in America, the *Pennsylvania Evening Post and Daily Advertiser*, began in 1783 in Philadelphia. At the outbreak of the Revolutionary War, there were 35 newspapers being published in the colonies. The first published west of the Appalachian Mountains was the *Pittsburgh Gazette* in 1786. *The Alexandria Gazette* (Virginia), published daily since 1797, is one of the oldest continuously published U.S. dailies.

A small, 80-cent classified advertisement appeared in the *Chicago Daily News* on April 1, 1887. It read:

> Watch-maker wanted – With references, who can furnish tools. State age, experience and salary required. Address T-39 Daily News.

When Richard Sears needed an assistant and Alvah Roebuck answered the ad and was hired, the world's largest retailer, Sears, Roebuck & Company, was born. It all started with a small advertisement in the newspaper and today Sears spends more than $417 million a year in newspaper advertising to perpetuate that small beginning.[5]

Along with the news that binds a community, a nation, or the world together, newspapers have always carried the advertisements that account for the livelihood of individuals and turn the wheels of commerce.

In the November 20, 1776 issue of the same *Essex Journal* which carried the account of Washington's defeat at the battle of White Plains and reported his army as being driven from Manhattan Island, this advertisement appeared: "A pig came to the farm of the subscriber about eight days ago, supposed to be about three months old. The owner may have him again by proving his property, paying the charges and applying to Samuel Emery of Newbury."

The *Pennsylvania Packet* of September 22, 1786 featured an article reporting the recommendation of John Dickinson, Alexander Hamilton, and James Madison that Congress call a federal convention to strengthen the Articles of Confederation leading to a new Constitution.

It also contained this advertisement: "Mr. Cenas takes this method to acquaint his friends and the public that he means to be in Philadelphia about the end of September and will open his Dancing School on the 3rd of October, from nine in the morning till one for Ladies and from four till nine for Gentlemen."

Newspaper employment continues to rank among the leaders of the nation's largest manufacturing employers. Revised Department of Labor statistics show an increase of 2,900 newspaper employees, from 421,900 in 1981 to 424,800 in 1982.[6]

Daily newspaper circulation increased to 62.4 million, more than 1 million above 1981 totals.

Newspaper advertising climbed to more than $18.3 billion, leading all major media with a 27.3 percent share of total advertising revenues.

Daily newspapers totaled 1,710 in number. There were 433 morning, 1,311 evening, and 34 "all day" newspapers.

Sunday newspaper totals reached a new high of 768, with circulation of more than 56.1 million.

The number of weekly newspapers was 7,626, with total circulation of 44.3 million. The average weekly newspaper circulation was 5,808.

Newsprint consumption as reported by all users was 10.1 million metric tons, with daily newspaper consumption estimated at 7.7 million metric tons, more than 76 percent of the total.

Newspapers are good business, too. In recent years in the nation's stock markets, newspaper stocks have outpaced the Dow Jones average consistently. That's why publishers last year alone invested $805 million in new equipment and plants. For the past five years, this amounts to over $3 billion.[7]

This involves new printing processes such as offset presses and full-color processing equipment, and satellite transmission of news and advertising matter.

The reporter writes the story and the person in the classified phone room actually sets the type that goes in the paper. They type into a video display terminal tied into a computer which hyphenates and regulates column width by driving the typesetting machines. Linotypes and their five column lines a minute of hot type have been replaced by cold type, photographically set at up to 1800 lines a minute.

Because computer typesetting does not have to be rekeyed by a mechanical worker, but goes directly from the writer to the finished typesetting, large numbers of mechanical employees are no longer required and cost savings have been effected. This allows publishers to engage more editorial employees for specialized writing to create a far more interesting product keyed to the local community.

The old "morgue" is now a computer data bank with instantly retrievable information. Offset presses produce higher quality newsprint, on the least expensive of all papers.

Newspapers require large numbers of people because of the near round-the-clock deadline nature of the product. They deal with large numbers of news sources, advertisers, and subscribers. Had publishers not been able to replace the plodding high-labor oriented, low-efficiency mechanical hot-type process with the high-speed, computerized cold-type system, the cost of newspapers for both subscriber and advertising would be out of sight.

Soon full-page pagination will enable newspapers to make up the entire page including all editorial, illustrations, photographs, and advertisements on a video screen, moving elements by use of a computer. There will not be any actual type either metal or photographic, only characters displayed on a tube.

By these huge investments and new techniques, newspapers are and will likely remain the cheapest way to get a large amount of information out to a mass audience.

Many newspapers are producing a weekly section delivered by carrier or mail to nonsubscribers. This is generally referred to as TMC or total market coverage. Thus, virtually every home can be reached in the newspaper's circulation area either by the regular subscriber product and/or a zoned edition going to subscribers, or a nonsubscriber section going to the full-circulation area or specific neighborhood zones within the overall circulation region.

And, newspapers are distributing pre-prints either by full circulation territory or by neighborhood zones. Pre-prints are full advertising sections printed in advance either by the newspaper or an outside printer, sometimes on a nationwide basis for a single store and inserted into the newspaper. They can go to all or part of the newspaper's subscribers or, if the paper has a nonsubscriber product, they can be inserted and distributed with it.

Another current advance in the industry is standardization of sizes. Until recently national advertisers were required to make up an ad in several different sizes to match the many column widths or page lengths. Now advertisers can buy standard advertising units (SAUs). There are at least 57 standard-sized units from which an advertiser can select. Well over 90 percent of the nation's dailies will be able to print it exactly the same size.

THE "BEST" NEWSPAPERS

Adweek, a journalism and telecommunication trade magazine, published a special report in April 1984 listing the best newspapers in the United States as picked by the following diverse panel of specialists:

David Cole, systems editor, *San Francisco Examiner* and former editor, *Feed Back*, the Northern California journalism review

Scott M. Cutlip, university professor of journalism and former dean of the School of Journalism, University of Georgia

Osborn Elliott, dean of the Columbia University Graduate School of Journalism and former editor of *Newsweek*

Everette Dennis, dean, University of Oregon School of Journalism

Jeff Greenfield, political analyst and media critic, ABC News

Daryl Moen, chairman, department of news-editorial, University of Missouri School of Journalism, Columbia

Ron Powers, media critic/commentator, CBS News

George Reedy, Neiman Professor of Journalism, Marquette University, Milwaukee

David Rubin, chairman of the Department of Journalism, New York University

Norman Sandler, White House correspondent, UPI

Paul E. Schindler Jr., Computer Systems News
David Shaw, media critic, *Los Angeles Times*
"a prominent industry observer"[8]

The list they picked in order of preference is as follows:

1. *The New York Times*
2. *The Washington Post*
3. *Los Angeles Times*
4. *The Wall Street Journal*
5. *The Miami Herald*
6. *The Philadelphia Inquirer*
7. *The Boston Globe*
8. *Newsday*
9. *Chicago Tribune*
10. (tie) *The Milwaukee Journal*
10. (tie) *Christian Science Monitor*

Not to be outdone, *Time* magazine published its own list of the "ten best U.S. dailies" also in April 1984. The *Time* list, it is assumed, was picked by its own panel of editors. *Time* published its list alphabetically with no order of preference.[9]

It is interesting to note that both lists are quite similar. *Adweek* lists *Newsday*, *The Milwaukee Journal* and *Christian Science Monitor* , which were not found in the *Time* list, and *Time* lists the *Des Moines Register* and *St. Petersburg Times*, which were not found in the *Adweek* list.

It should be noted that both of the above lists rate newspapers according to editorial excellence and do not take into consideration the business success or failure of any of the newspapers. However, as Mrs. Katharine Graham, chairman of the Washington Post Company has said on several occasions, it is almost impossible for a publication to be editorially excellent without enjoying success on the business side.

John J. Meskil, executive vice-president, media and administration, Warwick Advertising, states that 1984 was a year of golden opportunity for newspapers. Following are his viewpoints in the April 1984 issue of *Marketing and Media Decisions*:

The newspaper industry is making a concerted effort to obtain more advertising from national accounts.

But the question arises, can newspapers really hope to increase their national business and if so, how can they accomplish this?

Currently, newspapers receive about 8 to 10 percent of their business from National Accounts and 90 percent plus from local and classified advertising. Looking at this disparity one might ask, why should the newspapers care if they increase their national business since it represents such a small percentage of their total lineage? The answer to this is that national business is considerably more profitable than retail business. According to a recent 4A study, national advertisers pay 60 percent more than local advertisers for comparable space, so this is the area that newspapers would like to see their growth come from.

1983 was a good year for newspapers. Local ad spending increased with the ending of the recession and should continue this growth to an even greater degree in 1984. National business has been steady or declining but I can't remember a year in the past decade when newspapers were better situated to funnel national advertising dollars into the medium.

There are many reasons for my optimism:

• Newspapers have changed their look and their style of editing to appeal to a broader reader target. They can't fight television for instant news and they finally have begun to realize that. Color is being used more widely. *USA Today* has shown a good many publishers how attractive a newspaper can be by liberal use of color.

• For years, national advertisers have suffered through production problems. Sizes varied considerably from paper to paper, costing the advertiser considerable sums of money to meet each paper's requirements. A few years ago we thought we had finally solved the problem with the introduction of SAUs. But this failed miserably when only 49 percent of the papers cooperated.

Currently, newspapers have some 439 different ad sizes, but in July, this is all supposed to change. Dailies in the top 100 markets are expected to adopt the system of a standard newspaper page and depth measurement of inches rather than lines. This will eliminate lateral "float" and should eliminate production problems in these major market newspapers. This time I believe the newspaper industry will follow through with their decision, thus making the medium easier and less expensive to use.

There are several other factors which will enable newspapers to attract the national advertisers that have not heretofore been available:

• New research studies by SMRB and Scarborough which provide extensive demographic data in the top markets. The new studies confirm what we already assumed that newspaper readers are more upscale than television viewers and purchase a higher proportion of goods and services.

•   Of perhaps greater importance, the studies show larger readership than even the newspaper industry imagined: approximately 2.7 readers per copy. Previously, if the newspapers were given 2.0 readers per copy by agencies, they considered it generous.

•   Newspapers will be easier to compare with other media. The Newspaper Advertising Bureau has published a new booklet that is quite useful which translates newspaper readers into television rating points. If you don't have a copy, I suggest you contact the NAB and they'll be happy to send you one.

•   Television is sold out in almost all dayparts through the first half of the year, and even into the third quarter for news and daytime. Although I don't believe that newspapers can successfully sell against television as a replacement for national advertisers, they cannot help but benefit from this unusual condition. Advertisers will be looking to spend some of their advertising dollars that they could not place on television, and newspapers can be a valuable alternative. Like television, when you advertise in newspapers you get immediate response. Because of their timeliness and daily readership, advertisers can use newspapers to heavy up during critical sales periods for their brands.

If newspapers can prove to these advertisers that their sales were increased by this mix of television and newspapers, they should be able to retain some of this business if and when television returns to a "normal" sales pattern. In my opinion, the remainder of 1984 represents a golden opportunity for newspapers.

Finally, I sense a "feeling" among newspaper publishers that they are willing and anxious to change the poor image they have among many agencies and national advertisers. They have a perfect opportunity to sell accounts that they have heretofore not developed. They can broaden the type of accounts that normally might not have considered newspapers; accounts such as computers, new electronics technology and cable.

Ironically, I suspect newspapers will get more business over the next few years from cable advertisers hoping to increase audience than cable takes away from newspapers.

The key ingredient in newspapers' ability to attract national accounts is "sales." They must make a concerted effort to convince the advertising community that they really want national business and will make concessions to obtain it. They're off to a good start.[10]

NOTES

1. Public Affairs Department, American Newspaper Publishers Association, April 1983.

2. Bernard A. Weisberger, *The American Newspaperman,* pp. 1-3. Chicago, IL: The University of Chicago Press, 1961.

3. Ibid.

4. Ibid.

5. International Newspaper Advertising and Marketing Executives, Robert E. Cutler, chairman, Schools and Colleges Committee and Advertising Director, Salt Lake City Newspaper Agency Corporation. January 1984.

6. Ibid.

7. Ibid.

8. *Adweek*, "Special Report; Newspapers '84," April 1984, pp. 22-35.

9. *Time*, "The Ten Best U.S. Dailies," April 30, 1984, pp. 58-63.

10. "1984 – A Year of Golden Opportunity," John J. Meskil, executive vice-president, Warwick Advertising, *Marketing and Media Decisions,* April 1984, pp. 88-90.

2

CIRCULATION

Nothing can take the place of the intimate local contact enjoyed by a great newspaper. This was eloquently summed up in a piece of writing done by Frank Tripp, former chairman of Gannett Company, Inc.:

> When any medium other than the newspaper delivers all the world and neighborhood news in detail; ballyhoos local charities and civic endeavors to successful conclusions; borns the babies, graduates them, marries them; and buries them. . . . When it becomes the permanent record of current events; the date book of the community, the housewife's shopping guide; recovers the neighbor's dogs; sells their attics empty; finds them a used refrigerator; tells them who's sick, dead, engaged and married; who's painted his barn or mended his fences . . . then . . . I'll believe that some folks may not have time to read their hometown paper.[1]

Circulation in the newspaper business is the distribution of the newspaper to its readers. It is the number of newspapers sold and paid for through various sales methods. The most important are single-copy sales, mail distribution, and home delivery.

No matter how excellent the editorial product of the newspaper may be, its advertising revenue will be nonexistent if the newspaper is not sold and read. Circulation departments are becoming more and more vital to a newspaper's operation and are now accounting for 25 to 30 percent of newspapers' total revenue.

Today most large newspapers are operating under a marketing concept that coordinates the efforts of news advertising and circulation. Many newspapers have also appointed marketing directors, in many

11

The Arizona Republic/The Phoenix Gazette
Circulation Department Organizational Chart

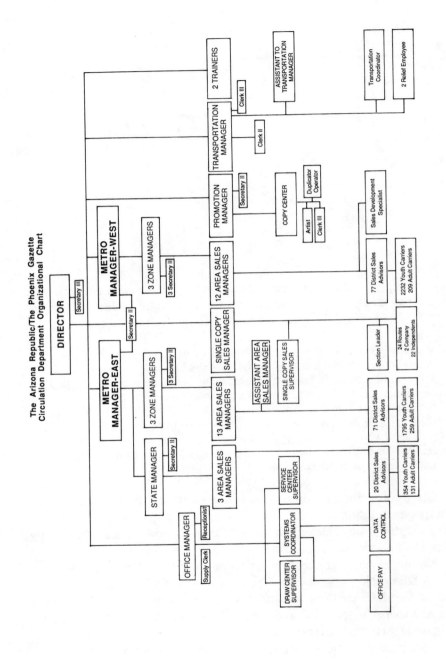

instances a vice-president, to whom both the advertising director and the circulation director report.

The main benefit of the modern marketing concept is that every department is working for, and should be an active participant in, its market. For most newspapers this is the "primary marketing area," a multicounty coverage measurement. This means working together as a team, with news, advertising, and circulation personnel sharing ideas and planning together.[2]

SINGLE-COPY SALES

Newspapers in the single-copy sales category are sold directly to street vendors at wholesale prices and they are then retailed to the buying public. The various outlets include newsstands, retail stores, newspaper boys on street corners, and street racks.

MAIL DISTRIBUTION

Non-daily newspapers depend on the U.S. Postal Service to deliver their newspapers more than daily newspapers. However, for those newspapers that do have mail subscribers, the postal method is still very efficient in spite of continuing increases in second-class postal rates.

HOME DELIVERY

Daily newspapers in most cities are delivered to the home by male or female carriers 12 years old and over. These carriers usually purchase the newspapers at the wholesale rate and deliver them to customers in a specified area at the retail price. The carriers are in a sense in business for themselves, and for years this operation has been known as the "Little Merchant Plan." In the suburbs and rural areas independent contractors, who are usually adults, deliver the newspapers by automobile or truck and either collect weekly, or the newspaper is paid for in advance at the home office.

All newspaper carriers are not 12 years old. Mr. B. C. Martin began delivering newspapers for the *Anniston* (Alabama) *Star* at the age of 35 and is still delivering them at the age of 82. He has 520 customers and is active seven days a week.[3]

CIRCULATION MANAGEMENT IDEAS

Circulation directors are usually aware of promotion and management ideas that help them in maintaining and increasing daily and Sunday circulation. Ronald C. Anderson, director of circulation for the Gannett newspapers in Rochester and New York, regularly outlines important management ideas in his column in the International Circulation Managers Association's *Update* publication:

---

1. *Sales Leads From Classified Department.* Overheard at a recent seminar in Wisconsin – one newspaper has its Classified Advertising system programmed to include a spot on the terminal menu screen for the ad taker to check whether or not the advertising customer subscribes to home delivery or not. Then, once a week, the Circulation Department receives a printout of all such advertisers who answered "no" to that question. It includes name, address and telephone number. Circulation's tele-marketing group then calls these people with excellent results.

2. *Direct Mail.* The Milwaukee newspapers have gone into direct mail marketing within the past year, and are realizing almost three percent positive response in selected suburban zone areas. They send a sales letter, miniature replica of the actual newspaper, and an order form. While cost per order is in the $12 range, they report excellent retention, which offsets the relatively high cost. They plan to intensify their direct mail marketing in 1984.

3. *Bowling As Carrier New Order Incentive.* The *Medina* (OH) *Gazette*, through an arrangement with a local bowling alley that wanted to build its family business, offered carriers three games of bowling, plus refreshments, for themselves and their families for one new order. Sounds like a *real* good value for just one new order!

4. *Mail Subscription Incentive.* A midwestern weekly newspaper, with 100 percent mail circulation, reported that one of its best promotions for new circulation was a recent in-paper offer to every subscriber for a six-month extension on their own subscription for each new order they obtained from someone else. A reader could earn a top limit of a two-year extension for four new orders sold.

5. *Public Promotion of Carrier Contest Winners.* At Beckley, West Virginia, carrier sales promotion participation is enhanced by publishing the results of each contest in the newspaper, so that the carrier's friends and neighbors can see what he or she won in the promotion.

6. *Carrier Service Incentive.* The *Morgantown* (WV) *Dominion Post* helps promote good service by carriers by rewarding one carrier in each district with a perfect service record for the month, with a breakfast outing with the District Sales Manager.

7. *Timely Price Item for Adult/Motor Route Carriers.* A telephone! In this time of personal ownership of telephone sets, some newspapers are successfully using this item to help generate order production from adults.

8. *Carrier Crewing Incentive.* At Gloversville, New York, carriers work extra hard during crewing to be the one who earns a $20 bill. In the crew, the first carrier to write an order is given the $20 bill. He or she gets to keep it until such time as one of the other carriers in the crew posts an order total ahead of this one. The bill keeps moving from carrier to carrier, always being held by the carrier with the current order production lead that day. At the end of crewing, the carrier with the most orders gets to keep the $20.

9. *Motor Route Sales Idea.* At Syracuse, New York, college students are used to follow-up motor route samples at the door. Sales results run as high as 25 percent of those sampled.

10. *Motor Route Delivery Idea.* The *Olean* (NY) *Times-Herald* periodically runs a computer mailing label printout of all motor route subscribers, so that drivers can maintain a sticker for each customer, just inside the front of each motor route tube. Helps in identification, especially when a substitute driver happens to be on.

11. *Back Copy Sales.* The *Holyoke* (MA) *Transcript-Telegram* frequently runs a special promotion ad which is really a back copy order coupon to cut out and mail in for prompt service on any back issues of the previous 12 months. Back copies of the 25 cent daily newspaper cost 40 cents and are mailed to ordering customers.

12. *Turkey Contest.* The *South Bend* (IN) *Tribune* ran a turkey for new orders promotion in the fall of 1983, but with an extra wrinkle. Carriers with points equivalent to three daily and Sunday orders got a 10 to 13 pound turkey, while those with points equivalent to five daily and Sunday orders won an 18 to 22 pound bird. The contest also featured a drawing for participants, in which four carriers each won $25 worth of groceries for the family Thanksgiving dinner.

13. *Direct Mail Offer.* The *South Bend Tribune* offered two hot/cold cups bearing the newspaper's logo, plus two individual servings of Maxwell House instant coffee for ordering a three-month home delivery subscription, either week-long, daily only, weekend-only, or Sunday-only.

Another direct mail campaign is directed to non-subscribers in towns that are featured in their Sunday roto magazine. Residents of these towns are mailed a special letter in advance, announcing the section on their town, and soliciting a half-price, three-month order. An attached flyer also promotes where the newspaper will be on sale there the day of the special section.

14. *Motor Route Expansion Idea. Watertown* (NY) *Daily Times* motor route drivers are given a copy of a form which can be filled out with information on potential additional motor route areas that are not yet being served and turn into circulation management for consideration. The form contains blocks for the name of the road(s), distance from nearest spot on present route, name of the nearest road on the present route, number of families living on the road, and the number of additional miles it would take to serve them. The form also ran in their carrier newsletter.

It strikes this writer as an idea that might also be worth working into a promotion ad for a newspaper interested in building its motor route operation – asking readers to suggest new areas where delivery expansion might be appropriate.

15. Converting Food-Day Customers to Week-Long Customers. Over the years, the Gannett Rochester (NY) newspapers have built extra home delivery customers on food advertising day totaling about 24,000. During the fall of 1983, a special marketing plan was put into place to convert as many of them as possible to week-long home delivery. Each such customer was identified with telephone numbers (where listed) on special sheets for telephone solicitors. For two weeks, one telephone sales crew called these people with a special offer – ten weeks of week-long *Times Union* or *Democrat & Chronicle* for 50 cents per week less than the regular price. Sales calls were made at the door, where appropriate. Also, flyers were inserted into single copy newspapers on food day, containing the same offer. Almost 1,600 new week-long daily orders resulted from this promotion – enough to convince us we should try it again midway through 1984 to try to swing more of these single-day customers to a more regular basis.

16. *Employee Sales Promotion.* The *Scranton* (PA) *Times* ran a special sales promotion for its employees during December 1983. Employees were offered a choice of a Christmas turkey or a $10 bill for each new 18-week, 7-day order they sold and turned in. Prospects were offered the first four weeks free, in the 18-week order. The same offer was made to the general public during this campaign, through a full-page ad in the newspapers. Readers were asked to sell for a commission,

while clubs, organizations, church and school groups were urged to sell subscriptions as a fund raiser.[4]

In total United States circulation, *The Wall Street Journal* leads all newspapers at 2,020,132 daily. The brand new *USA Today* is third in a list of the top 26 newspapers. The circulation of this newspaper has not been certified or filed with the Audit Bureau of Circulations in 1983 but was attested to by a reliable research firm.

1.	*The Wall Street Journal*	2,020,132
2.	*New York Daily News*	1,395,504
3.	*USA Today*	1,328,781 *
4.	*Los Angeles Times*	1,038,499
5.	*New York Post*	962,078
6.	*The New York Times*	910,538
7.	*Chicago Tribune*	751,024
8.	*The Washington Post*	718,842
9.	*The Detroit News*	650,683
10.	*Chicago Sun-Times*	639,134
11.	*Detroit Free Press*	635,114
12.	*The Philadelphia Inquirer*	533,176
13.	*San Francisco Chronicle*	530,954
14.	*Long Island Newsday*	525,216
15.	*The Boston Globe*	514,817
16.	*Cleveland Plain Dealer*	493,329
17.	*Houston Chronicle*	459,225
18.	*Newark Star-Ledger*	432,110
19.	*The Miami Herald*	406,656
20.	*The Houston Post*	402,181
21.	*Minneapolis Star & Tribune*	361,747
22.	*The Dallas News*	335,670
23.	*The Buffalo News*	318,667
24.	*Boston Herald*	317,612
25.	*Rocky Mountain News*	315,524
26.	*The Milwaukee Journal*	303,034

Source: USA Today statement average daily net paid circulation December 1983.

These are the latest available weekday figures as filed with the Audit Bureau of Circulation and are subject to audit (September 30, 1983 FAS-FAX [ABC Research]).

THE EFFECTIVE CIRCULATION EXECUTIVE

Thomas B. Sherrill, vice-president, marketing, of the Dispatch Printing Company, publishers of the *Columbus* (Ohio) *Dispatch*, and former president of the International Circulation Managers Association, had the following to say concerning his conception of an effective circulation executive:

The key to a successful circulation department and the only true barometer of an effective circulation executive is circulation increase. It is the job of the circulation executive to insure that the sales goals of the company are achieved. To accomplish these sales goals, the circulation executive must insure that sales calls are made, and in conjunction with this, provide the necessary promotional sales tools either through carrier incentive programs, creative sales approaches, intelligent use of marketing data, and the proper training and motivation of the sales force.

Good delivery service to the subscriber is of paramount importance. This dictates that service related policies must be subscriber oriented. Delivery systems must be designed for the customer's convenience and not for the company. For example, driveway delivery service compared to porch delivery. Another example is timely delivery of the product when the customer finds it most convenient to read, even at the expense of "late news." Service and circulation increase are directly correlated over the long run as excellent service makes selling much easier. Retention of the newspaper in the home ultimately depends on the type of service a subscriber receives. Circulation executives must also thoroughly understand the relationship between good delivery service and the image that good service generates in the eyes of an advertiser.

Circulation executives must maintain a hard-nosed approach to carrier collections. Good collection policies reflect in lower carrier turnover, fewer subscriber complaints, and fewer subscription cancellations, thus more sales and circulation increase. Good collections and effective management are synonymous. A circulation department cannot run smoothly unless collections are maintained at acceptable levels. Collection policies must be subscriber oriented. They must be designed for the customer's convenience and not only the company's profit desires. For example, forced office pay programs result in circulation loss because this collection policy is primarily for the company's convenience rather than for the convenience of the subscriber.

On expenses, circulation executives should "take care of the dollars and the pennies will take care of themselves." Since circulation departments are labor intensive, it is in the people area that circulation executives can make the most impact on controlling costs. Circulation executives must increase productivity with fewer people in order to survive in today's economy.

Circulation executives must be marketing executives. Being a distribution and order-getter expert no longer is sufficient in today's competitive marketplace. Circulation departments are no longer autonomous in their operation and they must coordinate their efforts with the advertising department in order to satisfy the wants and needs of the advertiser. They must become proficient in research and to learn to use this information properly to effectively compete with other media.[5]

ABC NEWSPAPER AUDIT REPORT

The Audit Bureau of Circulations (ABC) issues two types of reports on the circulations of each newspaper member – the semiannual Publisher's Statement, containing information supplied by the publisher and subject to audit, and the Audit Report, containing the findings of the ABC field auditor.

Audits are conducted annually with three exceptions:

1. Publishers of newspapers with less than 10,000 paid circulation who have exercised the option of a 24-month audit.
2. Weekly newspapers on the every-other-year audit plan.
3. Participants in weekly group audit plans where audits are made at least once every four years.

Each of these reports provides advertisers and advertising agencies with facts and figures on the quantity and quality of the newspaper's circulation. These represent a dependable basis for making advertising decisions.

In addition to supplying information such as how much circulation a newspaper has, and where and when it is distributed, ABC reports define the newspaper's market in terms of geographic areas, population, and households. To further assist the buyer in matching media to marketing needs, each of the ABC newspaper reports explains how the circulation was obtained, how much subscribers paid, circulation trends, and other clues to the quality of that circulation, distribution of the publication, and its stability within the market.

HOW MUCH CIRCULATION?

ABC breaks down the average paid circulation of the newspaper, showing the total distributed within each market area, usually by method of distribution used. Paid circulation distributed within each market area is directly related to the population and households of the area.

Distribution sold in lots of 11 or more is shown separately, along with other bulk sales. It is not included in either paid totals or the unpaid distribution.

The newspaper's Audit Report provides a further breakdown of an actual day's distribution in towns receiving 25 or more copies by counties. The detailed breakdown is reported by method of distribution as well as the amount so distributed, except for counties receiving less than 25 copies.

Collateral data are supplied in ABC newspaper reports so that circulation information can be directly related to households and population.

Where the newspaper's total distribution is broken down on an actual one-day performance basis, adjusted figures are provided so that the one-day's distribution can be related to average paid circulation for the period covered by the Audit Report.

For daily newspapers, ABC reports provide information on each edition, including press time, net press run, the approximate market area in which that run's production is distributed, and adjusted paid circulation for each run's production broken down by market areas.

Since trends and circulation growth are important in media evaluation, ABC Audit Reports give a four-year picture of the newspaper's average paid circulation.

CIRCULATION PROCUREMENT

Methods of circulation procurement are important in the qualitative evaluation of a newspaper's circulation. They answer the basic question, "How was the subscriber influenced to be a part of the audience of this newspaper?"

The ABC newspaper Audit Report and Publisher's Statement include an analysis of carrier and mail subscription sales in terms of production within the period covered by the report. Totals are given for premium, combination, and special offer sales; clubs; contests; insurance plans, and arrears under three months. Shown also are the prices charged within various market areas for each type of distribution.

Wherever special subscription inducements are used, ABC makes a complete explanation of the publisher's offer.[6]

INTERNATIONAL CIRCULATION MANAGERS ASSOCIATION

The International Circulation Managers Association is located at Newspaper Center in Reston, Virginia. It is headed by Joseph B. Forsee, who is the general manager.

A small group of publishers, and advertising and circulation managers met in Detroit, Michigan, on November 23, 1898 to organize the National Association of Newspaper Circulation Managers. The charter group of circulators consisted of only 35 members.

The first annual convention was held in Chicago, Illinois in June 1899, and by 1905 the Association had grown to 139 members. In 1915 the membership totaled 305 and today the Association has a membership of over 1,350. In 1910 the Association grew beyond the boundaries of the United States into Canada and overseas and became international in scope.

The purpose of the Association is to provide circulation executives with effective and continuous leadership; to report to the members the most efficient methods for the marketing, in its broadest concept, of daily newspapers for the mutual benefit of the public, newspaper publishers, and circulation personnel; and to provide for the circulation, education, and information of its regular members.

There are four classes of memberships: regular, associate, honorary, and honorary life. The general manager reports to a board of directors consisting of 16 circulation directors from member newspapers elected for various terms of office.

Seventeen committees serve the membership throughout the year. Members of these committees are appointed by the president of the association, who is elected by the membership. Under the president is an executive vice-president, a first vice-president, and a second vice-president.

One of the most interesting committees to educators is the Newspaper in Education Committee. This committee stimulates interest among members to participate in education programs in both high schools and colleges.

ICMA Update is the Association's monthly magazine, and features news, ideas, and helpful hints. It is the only publication of the industry devoted exclusively to circulation. The author recently served on the *Update* editorial board.

NEWSPAPER CIRCULATIONS SET NEW RECORDS

In the summer of 1983 new research revealed that newspaper readership had increased from 2.2 readers per copy to 2.7 readers, or about 20 percent. In January 1984 the Audit Bureau of Circulations announced in its annual study that total daily circulation as of September 30, 1983 had increased to a record high of 63.1 million copies, or one and a half percent over the same figure for the previous year.

What is not reported is that this gain on top of the gain made the previous year adds up to an increase in daily copies sold of 1.7 million or 2.8 percent over the last two years.

There was a shift in circulations and newspapers from the evening field, which showed a circulation loss of 2.9 percent, to the morning field, which showed a gain of 7 percent, but the daily total was up, as was the Sunday circulation figure. Sundays set new records in number of newspapers (758) as well as total circulation (56.3 million, for a 2.3 percent gain).

As readership and circulation led the way, advertisers followed, and newspapers set new records for advertising revenues in 1983 with every classification showing large gains, especially classified advertising.

All of this has taken place when the newspaper business was going through some contractions in the major cities and while the nation was coming out of a major recession. It shows – especially the circulation increases – the increasing reliance of the American people on their newspapers for news and other information forecasting a growing and healthy future for print media in this country.[7]

NOTES

1. Frank Tripp, *Gannetteer*, May-June 1984, front cover.
2. D. Earl Newsom, *The Newspaper*, p. 152. Englewood Cliffs, NJ: Prentice-Hall, 1981.
3. "Letters to the Editor," *Editor & Publisher*, January 7, 1984, p. 7.
4. Circulation Management Ideas, Ronald C. Anderson, director of circulation, Gannett Rochester New York Newspapers, *ICMA Update*, December 1983, January 1984, pp. 17, 18.
5. Personal interview with Thomas B. Sherrill, vice-president, the Dispatch Printing Company, February 7, 1984.
6. "How To Read A Newspaper Audit Report," March 1984, Audit Bureau of Circulations, Schaumburg, IL.
7. *Editor & Publisher*, January 21, 1984, p. 6.

3

GENERAL MANAGEMENT

A free press must be fortified with greater knowledge of the world and skill in the arts of expression.
–S. I. Newhouse, August 5, 1964
Syracuse University, Syracuse, New York

The approach here will be confined to how newspaper management is structured, how, generally, it functions, and what some of the philosophies governing it are. Additionally, some insights into the problems and opportunities it faces will be offered.

MANAGING AS AN ART

Despite the fact that management may be "a body of knowledge that can be studied and practiced";[1] despite the fact that many, if not most managers have been schooled in management theory and techniques to one degree or another, management (particularly newspaper publishing management) remains an art. The origins, experience, or expertise individuals achieve in the various disciplines from which they emerged to join the ranks of management do not necessarily qualify them for the positions they hold. Throughout the entire history of newspaper publishing, it has been repeatedly evident that success as a sales or marketing person, an accountant, or a circulation professional does not automatically guarantee equivalent success as a manager.

24

The missing ingredient is often the ability to effect what Dr. Karen R. Gillespie, in her recent book, refers to as "creative supervision," a term that has also been defined as the process of organizing and employing resources to accomplish a predetermined objective with and through people.[2] Expressed another way, the science of management can be taught; the art of management, if not bestowed by nature, must be learned.

There is a body of opinion that hold that newspaper publishing demands more varied abilities of its executives than does almost any other calling. Successful newspaper executives not only have to be effective managers, but they also must possess creative ability or, at least, the capacity to work with creative people; they must have the talent for salesmanship and the feeling for promotion and publicity usually associated with sales skills; and they must have a familiarity with the technical aspects of printing and production.[3]

Most experts agree that managers usually perform five basic functions: planning, organizing, directing, coordinating, and controlling. The emphasis placed on these functions varies by the requirements of the position that utilizes them, but all of them are essential in the management operation, and all are embodied in one form or another in the nature of a company's corporate culture.

ABOUT CORPORATE CULTURE

Regardless of its size or industry classification, every company has some kind of corporate culture which, as noted by Terrence E. Deal and Allan A. Kennedy in *Corporate Culture*, comprises "the rites and rituals of corporate life."[4]

In a *Fortune* magazine article on management, Bro Utte, summing up the themes of a number of books on the subject, defines corporate culture as

> . . . a system of shared values (what is important) and beliefs (how things work) that interact with a company's cultural transition.[5]

In the end, however, *managing* demands *managers*, and it is thus important to assess the types of positions managers hold, the roles they must play, and their fit within the organizational structure.

TABLE OF ORGANIZATION OF A TYPICAL LARGE DAILY NEWSPAPER

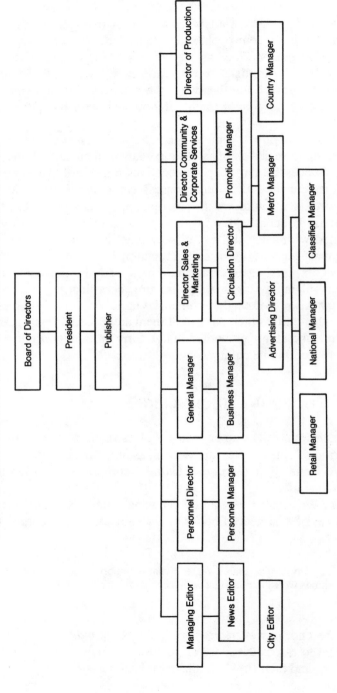

THE STRUCTURE OF MANAGEMENT

According to Peter F. Drucker, managers practice management. A manager must make decisions under conditions of uncertainty and, above all, must be adept at strategic planning. One who is schooled only in skills and techniques and fails to grasp the fundamentals of management is not a manager, but, at best, a technician.[6]

A well-coordinated newspaper venture encompasses eight major departments: editorial, advertising, circulation, manufacturing (production), marketing, promotion, research, and of course, administration, which in the author's definition, includes finance and, in the case of larger publishing houses, information systems. Other departments, while extremely important, relate less to the actual publishing of the newspaper than to essential staff activities. These include corporate communications, which embraces public affairs and publicity, personnel, and legal services.

Many newspaper publishing companies today are highly complex organizations. They may publish a number of newspapers within a corporate publishing group while having, at the same time, commitments in such diverse areas as broadcasting, real estate, forest lands, printing companies, and distribution operations. In the interest of clarity and simplicity, discussion in this chapter will be confined to the management structure of an archetypical, large-circulation daily newspaper. Following are job descriptions of managers of all operating departments, and selected staff departments.

President

The president, who may also function as the chief executive officer, usually reports to the chairman of the board and the board of directors. This office is critical. It is, first and foremost, responsible for the profit and loss position of the company. It is also responsible for the direction of the entire company, from developing long-term strategy to assuring the compliance of actions consistent with it.

The management and development of the existing operation is but one part of the job. In recognition of the fact that "if you stand still, you may be run over," the president also must explore and capitalize on opportunities for appropriate expansion, and act decisively to eliminate inappropriate operations.

With a top management team, the president must develop and maintain standards of corporate quality; ensure that the entire staff is highly motivated, well trained, and equitably compensated; and, further, that continuity of values, growth, and success is assured by the presence in depth of qualified top and middle management.

Because of the importance of the revenue derived from the sale of advertising, the president must develop and maintain contact with day advertisers and their agencies.

Publisher

Traditionally, at most newspapers, the publisher is the chief operating officer responsible for profits and editorial excellence through the development of an appropriate strategy, and sees that various service groups execute specific tactics for the most effective support of the entire effort. In recent years, publishers have been selected from business as well as the editorial operation.

Possibly because in journalism history, particularly that of newspapers, one person often fulfilled the dual role of editor and publisher, there exists some confusion about the extent to which one function affects the other in today's world, where the publisher and the editor in most instances have discrete roles. As noted, the editorial operation is usually quite distinct from the business operation, a form of separation frequently equated to that existing between "church and state" by many in newspaper publishing. In practice, the publisher, whose responsibilities are business centered, and the editor, whose primary concerns are reader oriented, may, from time to time, find themselves in adversary positions. When such situations do arise, the president may be called on to adjudicate them. In the end, difficulties are usually resolved to the best interests of the newspaper as a whole.

Advertising Director

Publishing has its own lexicon, and one of its oddities is revealed in the designation of the top newspaper sales job. Although the more descriptive title would be *advertising sales director*, the position is almost universally called simply *advertising director*. (Curiously, the person usually charged with responsibility for the company's advertising is not

given an advertising soubriquet, but is known as the *promotion director.*)
Essentially, the advertising director directs the publication's entire
advertising space sales operation, as well as that of the marketing or
advertising services group. A more detailed analysis of the position's
responsibilities will be presented in the chapter on sales and marketing
management, to follow later.

Circulation Director

As the second largest source of a newspaper's revenue, circulation,
which generates income from the sales of copies to both subscribers and
newsstand buyers, is an extremely important element in the newspaper's
business structure. It is the duty of the circulation director to maintain the
circulation base (on which the rates that management charges advertisers
for advertising space is predicated), and to generate the quality of
subscribers, in quantity, in the most cost-efficient manner possible. A
further requirement is to enlarge the circulation rate base without loss of
quality or efficiency, if circumstances dictate the need for a broader
readership.

A basic responsibility is, naturally, the distribution of the newspaper
– the ways and means by which subscriber copies are put in readers'
hands in a timely manner – and newsstand copies are delivered to
distributors' whole-field sales forces, which in turn see to it that
newsstands are well stocked and serviced.

In addition to having to keep abreast of a reading public that is
constantly changing in dynamics, size, and composition, the circulation
director has to assess and deal with myriad unpredictable variables, from
changing government regulations and varying economic factors to the
vagaries of the weather which, when inclement, might seriously impede
delivery of the newspaper to readers. The circulation director must also
be well versed in the principles of circulation acquisition (the methods by
which circulation is developed) and fulfillment (the servicing of
subscription orders and subscriber needs). In addition to having a high
degree of promotion expertise and a solid financial background, the
circulation director must also become thoroughly familiar with the rules,
regulations, and by-laws of the Audit Bureau of Circulations, the
industry-sponsored watchdog of newspaper and magazine circulation
practice.

Production Director

Often called the *director of manufacturing* in large newspapers, the production director is the person who sees to it that the editorial matter and the advertisements come together and are printed, bound, and readied for distribution each week or month. Some production managers are responsible for the purchase and inventory of newsprint, the paper on which newspapers are printed, as well as for negotiating printing agreements and developing and maintaining the company's manufacturing abilities.

The cost of the three P's, the primary source of newspaper publishing outlay – paper, printing, and postage – have been advancing more rapidly than other costs in recent years. These developments place enormous pressure on production directors to ensure that the materials and techniques used in the manufacturing process are the most efficient available to handle the gargantuan task of producing numerous geographic, demographic, and special editions of a newspaper, with dispatch.

Given the advances in photocomposition, satellite transmission, and laser printing, the job of production director has increased in significance over the years.

Other Managers

In an era that has seen the emergence and steady growth of an information society, the creation, storage, manipulation, and transmission of data have become vital necessities, nowhere more so than in the publishing industry which literally depends on information for existence. It is a natural development, then, that the processing of information and the management of its applications to problem solving and accomplishing tasks in a faster, more economical, and more accurate manner require special knowledge and talents. These attributes fall within the province of the *director of information systems*, whose function it is to create, maintain, and improve technical methods and systems and provide information useful to the achievement of the newspaper's objectives, whether short- or long-term in character.

The *financial officer* is the indispensable key to the management of a newspaper's financial, planning, and accounting policies and practices who keeps an eye on general business aspects. This individual is generally closely allied with the president's office, as the chief monitor to the corporate profit and loss position.

The *director of communication* is another who is closely connected with the front office, charged with counseling and supporting the president in all matters relating to both the external and the internal perceptions of the newspaper. In so doing, this person is involved in all areas of public affairs and publicity. Specifically, the job entails the direction of the public relations, or publicity, manager who plays a major role in developing and maintaining favorable relations with the press; of corporate events like company meetings and outings and top-level entertainment or seminar events; and of the contact person in industry and community relations.

The communications director also functions as the liaison between the editorial and business staffs when it is advantageous to the newspaper to involve both in business situations, such as those requiring an editor to speak at an outside industry affair. In many newspapers, the publishing of a "house organ" also falls within the communications director's purview.

In addition to being responsible for company hiring, the *personnel director* advises management on a wide variety of personnel-related issues, keeps abreast of government regulations affecting personnel practices, monitors corporate adherence to policies such as the affirmative action plan, and oversees relations with various unions. Employee benefits, including insurance, health care, vacation, and retiree programs are other areas of concern to this office.

In Summary

While the above outline provides what has been described as an example of a "typical" newspaper management structure, the fact is that few companies conform to structure types per se. Moreover, as a company evolves, its needs usually change, and it tends to modify its structure to meet the new circumstances. What does tend to remain constant and, indeed, to govern the performance of a newspaper is the philosophy of its management.

MANAGEMENT PHILOSOPHY

If, as had been stated, management is an art, it follows that managers are artists. And like artists, each is an individual, differing from the next in greater or lesser ways. They judge similar, often the same, sets of facts from different perspectives. They wield their brushes in differing manners, using diverse metiers of expression. They produce varied results within different time frames. All of this is to say that there are as many philosophies of management as there are managers and that one is not necessarily better than another. If the application of a philosophy to the realities of a company's situation produces the desired results, the philosophy is obviously right for the manager articulating it.

Some common threads do seem to weave through the philosophies of different managers. For example, they seem to share a belief that the need to attract, motivate, properly compensate, and retain good employees is fundamental to successful management. Another area of commonality is seen in their desire to create an environment in which risk-taking is encouraged, a climate that fosters a high level of thinking, a willingness to venture new ideas, and a conviction that doing so will prove psychologically, if not necessarily financially, rewarding for both employees and the company.

Edward W. Estlow, president, Scripps-Howard, expressed his concept of what constitutes good business management in the newspaper industry in a personal interview:

Today we are in the midst of one of the most extensive communications revolutions since Gutenberg created the printing press. Its cause has been automation, and particularly the computer. It has created whole new enterprises in communications and entertainment.

A few years ago we in the media were mainly concerned with newspapers, radio and television. Today we are dealing with those three plus cable television, videotext, teletext, cellular radio, satellite transmission, etc. It takes a tremendous amount of time and effort for a newspaper executive to keep up with the technology and the extensive demands of government for control and reporting.

The amount of time consumed to keep informed is staggering.

But, without being informed, planning is impossible – and it is critical if survival and progress are to be attained in the newspaper business.

Thirty or forty years ago practically no planning took place on any newspaper. Profit margins were so handsome little thought was needed in the long range direction.

This whole scene has changed radically. If a newspaper is to survive and show good progress today it must have an annual plan and a strategic (long range) plan or failure will result over the course of time.

This planning requires a newspaper to be in tune with its community. It requires a product of quality to meet consumer demands. It requires newspapers to re-define their markets in order to capture advertising. It requires a degree of financial management unheard of twenty years ago. It requires constant upgrading of productivity and it requires delivery of product at the time the consumer demands it.

All this, plus reasonable cash flow, financial resources and product creativity should spell success.[7]

Katharine Graham, chairman of the board and CEO of the Washington Post Company, puts it another way:

I would like to say that rising to the marketing challenge we face today is essential. Advertising is the lifeline of the print medium. Without it the free press as we know it would fast disappear. But to my way of thinking, winning the war for ad dollars is not enough. Our public trust goes deeper. It compels us to provide quality news to as many people as we can reach. Attempting to fulfill this responsibility will take the best we can give in hard work, creative thinking, and deep commitment, but if we lose sight of this larger duty, if we take the easy way out, we will fail not only our readers and advertisers, but ourselves and our country.[8]

Darrow "Duke" Tully, publisher of *The Arizona Republic* and *The Phoenix Gazette*, states that "good business management" of a newspaper is not very subjective. In his opinion it consists of the following axioms, which have proven successful in all of the major newspapers he has operated over the years:

A. To return a decent profit to the stockholders, i.e., somewhat in excess of a no-risk return investment in government securities.

B. Building towards a current asset/current liability ratio of approximately two to one. This will provide enough cash reserves to carry the newspaper over any temporary rough spots.

C. Constant favorable comparison with other newspapers in comparable circulation/revenue categories (for instance, if a newspaper in your peer group is recognized as one of the better newspapers in the United States, how do your expenses, by department, break down as a percentage of total expenses. This simple exercise will indicate whether you are spending enough on the product or being wasteful in the production area.)

D. A viable employee relations program based around a fair and equitable wage and salary program is essential. Openness about job requirements and expected rate of pay in all categories is a great morale booster and constant comparisons with circulation peer groups will prove to your employees that they are being fairly treated.

E. A well balanced internal communication program consisting of such things as: a company newspaper, supervisor lunches with the publisher, coffee with the publisher for random groups of employees, adequate bulletin boards throughout the building for posting of new jobs and for reminders about company or corporate developments of interest to the employee.

F. A well articulated MBO program encompassing all executives, directors, managers and supervisors with quarterly checks to let them know how they are doing.[9]

As pointed out in the beginning of this chapter, managing is an art. Over the years I have found some important precepts that have been very helpful. I would like to share them with my readers:

1. Determine ahead of time what you are trying to accomplish in the managing job.

2. Remind yourself that all the people with whom you work have desires important to them.

3. Find out the specific wants of those with whom you work.

4. Make these desires a part of your repertory of management tools to be used with vigor and judgment to further your own progress toward your selected goal.

5. Successful managers tend to be people who want to influence and control other people in order to get organizational work done, not in order

to glorify themselves.

6. Often a major problem attaining successful managerial goals is simple lack of sensitivity for other people on the part of the manager.

7. Learn to develop self-confidence in order to ward off frustrations that lead managers to aggressive reactions.

8. People directing an organized human effort must necessarily spend some of their time making judgments about the fitness of certain members for certain tasks. This is a skill requiring effort and practice, and also requiring the absence of certain personality blocks.

9. In managing, communication is a primary tool for effecting behavior change. Two-way communication between manager and employee has the advantages of greater accuracy and greater feelings of certainty for the receiver.

10. A manager must keep the flow of events from determining what he or she does, what he or she works on, and what he or she takes seriously, otherwise an executive will fritter himself away "operating." He or she needs criteria which enable the manager to work on the truly important, that is, on contributions and results.

11. Effective executives know what they expect to get out of a meeting, a report, or a presentation; and what the purpose of the occasion is or should be. They ask themselves, "Why are we having this meeting?"

12. A superior has responsibility for the work of others, as well as power over their careers. Making the strengths of an organization productive is therefore much more than an essential of effectiveness. It is a responsibility of authority and position.

13. Restrictive authority is seen by managers as a tool for coordination and control. It is simple and fast. One of the difficulties is that restriction may come from frustration and may be followed by aggression toward the executive.

According to Leo Bogart, executive vice-president, Newspaper Advertising Bureau, daily newspaper publishers and editors today face tasks and problems that are varied and demanding. They must accommodate themselves to a new era in their own production technology and at the same time anticipate changes in the technology of electronic home communications that will affect newspapers profoundly. They must battle new restrictions to the flow of news, that are imposed or threatened by foreign governments and created domestically by the courts. They must meet the political questions inevitably raised by the growing weight of groups and multimedia conglomerates within their business. But most important they must consider how their newspapers should change to resume circulation growth at a pace that matches their potential. Such growth is essential for any medium to remain vital and strong.[10]

NOTES

1.　Randall Poe, "A Walk and Talk with Peter Drucker," *Across the Board,* February 1983, p. 32.

2.　Karen R. Gillespie, *Creative Supervision,* p. 6. New York: Harcourt Brace Jovanovich, 1981.

3.　William H. Scherman, *How to Get the Right Job in Publishing,* pp. 65, 66. Chicago, IL: Contemporary Books, 1983.

4.　Terrence E. Deal and Allan A. Kennedy, *Corporate Cultures,* p. 1. Reading, MA: Addison-Wesley, 1983.

5.　Bro Utte, *Management,* "The Corporate Culture Vultures," *Fortune,* October 17, 1983, p. 66.

6.　Peter F. Drucker, *Management,* p. 17. New York: Harper & Row, 1974.

7.　Personal interview with Edward W. Estlow, president, Scripps-Howard, Los Angeles, CA, November 9, 1983.

8.　Katharine Graham, chairman, Washington Post Company, address delivered to the 1983 Annual Conference of the Audit Bureau of Circulations, Century Plaza Hotel, Los Angeles, CA, November 9, 1983.

9.　Personal interview with Darrow "Duke" Tully, publisher, The *Arizona Republic/Phoenix Gazette,* Phoenix, AZ, April 16, 1984.

10.　Leo Bogart, *Press and Public,* p. 1. Hillsdale, N.J.: Lawrence Erlbaum Associates, 1981.

4

ADVERTISING SALES

Nothing ever happens until Something is Sold! Whatever man invents, discovers, makes, grows, or performs might just as well never have been invented, discovered, manufactured, grown or performed if nobody steps up to buy it!! Everything we use today – goods, services or ideas – first had to be Sold. The billions of dollars spent annually by men, women and children, for all manner of goods, services, and ideas, are the cumulative result of selling that dates back to earliest recorded history.[1]

– Raymond McKinney, former president,
J. P. McKinney & Sons, former advertising
representative firm for the Gannett Company,
October 6, 1944

A newspaper is a unique product. Unlike packaged products or hard goods, it must continually change its appearance. Every day, it must look different enough to attract repeat buyers at the newsstands, but not so different that its identity is lost or blurred.

It is not surprising, then, that the world of advertising sales is one of seeming contradictions, often confusing to the uninitiated. Consider, for example, that an advertising salesperson literally does not sell the product he or she represents. That product, the newspaper, is actually sold to subscribers and to newsstand buyers by the circulation department. What the advertising representative does sell is a concept: advertising in the newspaper will reach an audience of a size, composition, and demography that conforms to the advertiser's definition of the marketplace of people comprising the best customers and prospects for the product or service to be sold – at a price the advertiser is willing to pay.

The concept is complicated on two counts. First, the representative sells only white space in the newspaper; it is the advertiser's responsibility to create and produce the advertising that appears in that space. Therefore, the advertising representative has no control over the content or quality of the advertising produced. Second, the "audience" of a newspaper is ephemeral, while its base is the actual circulation of the newspaper, that is, the combined number of its subscription and newsstand buyers, as audited by the Audit Bureau of Circulations.

ADVERTISING SALES REPRESENTATIVE

Far from being the stereotype of the "hail fellow well met" entertainer envisioned by the unknowledgeable, a sales representative is as close to being an entrepreneur as anyone who works for a corporation can be, a concept that will be addressed in greater detail later.

It is an adage of selling that "people like to do business with people they like," and although it is true that personal relationships can and sometimes do influence a buyer's decision, the decision ultimately rests on the quality of the salesperson's newspaper and of the audience it serves. Generally speaking, it is only when newspapers of relatively equal effectiveness are competing for the same piece of business that the buyer can afford the luxury of favoring one representative over another.

SALESPERSON AS ENTREPRENEUR

The concept of salesperson as entrepreneur springs from the businesslike manner in which sales efforts are conceived and executed. Typically, each salesperson is assigned a number of accounts along with the complete responsibility for both selling and servicing them. In so doing, the representative must know and understand the dynamics of the industries in which his accounts fall; the competitive forces at work within them; the marketing, sales, and advertising objectives of each; and their infrastructures. Those influential in the decision-making hierarchy must be identified, categorized by the degree of influence, and regularly called on and given pertinent information and data. Thus, the representative might spend a morning keeping an advertising agency's media staff aware of the newspaper's status, progress, and plans, and feeding that group new or differently presented information on its audience's appropriateness for the advertiser's product. Later, the representative might visit with the agency executives managing the account, ending the day at dinner with their client's advertising manager or some higher executive. In short, a newspaper salesperson must develop and maintain cordial relationships with those on every level of agency and client company structure.

According to Vance Stickell, executive vice-president, marketing, of the *Los Angeles Times,* there are five important precepts to keep in mind concerning good sales management in the newspaper business.

One, the selection of people. I look for people that I believe can act, look and represent *The Times* on their own. They may be the only representative a customer will see from *The Times* . . . so, the question becomes, will that person be a good ambassador, projecting the proper image and creditable sales story for this newspaper.

Two, as managers are we furnishing that individual with the sales tools necessary to tell our story thoroughly so that we are providing ideas that will not only result in revenues for us, but are the best for the customer. Can those suggestions result in a partnership that is truly equitable and profitable to both the customer and *The Times.*

Three, does the sales individual have the proper compensation balance of security and incentive. That individual must be motivated to earn at the highest practical level, but at the same time have a sufficiently good base salary so that the pressures of rent and grocery expenses are not distracting.

Four, as managers have we spelled out the objectives for the individual. Does he or she know precisely what is expected and what the rewards are if those goals are achieved. Conversely, do they know what the penalties are if the goals are not reached. MBO (Management by Objectives) techniques are applied here at *The Times* . . . but goal setting need not be that formalized as long as the salesperson understands what management expects.

Five, recognition beyond financial rewards, in the form of a telephone call, a handwritten memo, a word in the elevator or hallway, is important. They let the individual know that you, as a manager, are really aware of their activities. Even the most secure, successful salesperson has moments of doubt, even loneliness. They often wonder if management really knows how hard they're working and if anybody really cares. That's why any personal message, no matter how brief or informal, can help the sales manager maintain good morale. And, obviously, there is nothing like the four-legged call when the manager goes out into the field to listen, help and observe.[2]

INDUSTRY CATEGORY SYSTEM

Keeping abreast of the developments in a group of industries is a demanding requirement. In order to ensure that their sales representatives have access to the most information available as well as guidance from those with more specialized knowledge of a given industry, many newspaper advertising departments have adopted some kind of an industry category system.

The industry category approach to advertising sales generally takes one of two forms. In the first instance, individuals having concentrated experience or expertise in a particular industry may act informally as centralized information sources for their associates to draw on. These people may accompany other salespeople on calls, contributing to the advertiser insights and perceptions derived from their wealth of experience. Other, and usually larger, newspapers establish a well-defined system in which major advertising classifications have assigned supervisors. In practice, these people tend to manage information as well as other people, and their responsibilities include attendance at important industry conventions, the monitoring of the industry trade press for applicable news and ideas, the dissemination of ideas and information to concerned salespeople, and the development of wide-ranging, multilevel contact with companies in their categories, and with their advertising agencies.

ADVERTISING DEPARTMENT STRUCTURE

The size and complexity of a newspaper's advertising department structure depends on the size of the publication; whether it functions as a sole entity or as part of a newspaper group; and the number of advertising classifications from which it solicits business. Smaller newspapers and weekly newspapers may require correspondingly fewer sales representatives to cover their customers and prospects. A large newspaper's sales force may consist of as many as 60 or 70 retail representatives, the same number of classified advertising representatives, and four or five in national.

In this chapter, the management structure of a large, single-entity newspaper will be discussed. Such a structure normally consists of an advertising director, to whom retail and a national manager and, frequently, the promotion director and the research director report. Although the promotion and research directors report to the advertising director in some companies, in others they report to the publisher for reasons that will be explained later.

An understanding of the duties of some of these managers is critical to the understanding of how an advertising sales force operates.

Marketing Director

Many large daily newspapers in the past ten years have instituted a new top-level position in newspaper advertising sales. This position has the title of marketing director, director of sales and marketing, or just director of sales. The position usually carries a vice-president designation, and in some cases executive vice-president. The person in this position has pursued the route of advertising sales, although in some cases the executive has risen through the circulation department ranks. This executive is in charge of advertising sales, circulation, promotion, marketing, and research.

Advertising Director

The advertising director is accountable for the direction of all advertising sales and services operations of the newspaper and for the development of maximum advertising sales revenues.

A primary concern of the advertising director is the need to attract, motivate, train, and manage the sales and services staffs in a manner that ensures the most productive utilization of their abilities and creates a pool of talent that ensures a line of competent management succession.

The advertising director has a host of corollary duties. To name but a few of them, this person must:

Allocate sales and services resources productively. This means making the most effective use of available people and dollars, seeing to it that the sales effort is most concentrated where the greatest business potential is.

Forecast and monitor advertising pages and revenue potential. Advertising sales and services operating budgets are predicated on the estimated number of pages the sales staff feels can be sold in the fiscal year. It is therefore essential that page estimates be as accurate as possible and that deviations from it, plus or minus, be registered with general management.

Identify and develop new sources of revenue. Advertising is not a static industry. Businesses are born, grow, mature, and either die or remain on a plateau, their potential as sources of advertising revenue varying accordingly. The advertising director must keep close tabs on their status; sense and uncover new opportunities; and direct staff efforts to growth areas. At some newspapers, this function is also a primary concern of the marketing director.

Maintain high-level contact at major advertising companies and agencies. The advertising director usually has a broader view of advertising situations and, as a result of a national exposure, a greater personal awareness of the commonality of problems and their solutions. Moreover, this person, having greater access to company policy and wider decision-making authority than a line salesperson, can remain firm or make a concession in a negotiating situation, in a way that the line salesperson cannot. The cachet of the title also gives the advertising director access to a company at higher echelons of management.

Finally, the advertising director is the focus of all the activities, of whatever degree of importance, that crowd into a sales organization day. In a business having a high turnover of people, as advertisers switch agencies and agencies adjust their staffs accordingly, and as client and agency people switch companies or move within their own companies to assume different responsibilities, the advertising director has to maintain personal relationships in frequently changing contexts. Internally, he or she faces the necessity of resolving both the business and the personal problems that are an integral part of managing a staff of sensitive, articulate, competitive individuals. Additionally, there are customer complaints about the position of their advertisement in the newspaper and the quality of the advertisement's reproduction; the unusual demands for special advertising configurations; and myriad other situations to be confronted in the course of an average day.

Promotion Director

Whereas the advertising director is, in practice, the sales director of a newspaper, the promotion director is its true advertising manager. For this position, usually in conjunction with the company's advertising agency, is responsible for the newspaper's advertising in consumer and trade publications, in outdoor media, with larger newspapers, and on television and radio.

An unusual dichotomy exists within this position, and it explains why, at some newspapers, the promotion director reports to the publisher rather than to the advertising director. The fact is that the promotion director often has to serve conflicting interests. The publisher may want the advertising to communicate a certain image of the newspaper and of the publishing company itself – advertising that positions the newspaper in a general way as one of singular editorial excellence, or as an industry leader and innovator, a major contributor to the advancement of the advertising industry as a whole. This kind of advertising is intended also to create an aura of statesmanship about the newspaper and provide an "umbrella" of advertiser acceptance under which the field sales force can operate, secure in the knowledge that the advertising has created a set of "credentials" for them.

The advertising director, on the other hand, may prefer more specific, more immediately sales-oriented advertising that conveys the newspaper's basic selling strengths to the advertising community. Such things as advertising line and revenue leadership, demographic superiority, cost-efficiency advantages, award-winning editorial and outstanding circulation performance are all topics the sales force would like to see constantly being reiterated in advertising.

The promotion director, as the one executing the advertising, must satisfy both requirements. What often happens is that the job develops as a two-pronged one. The publisher will concentrate on the advertising in consumer and major advertising industry media, while the advertising director's philosophy will largely prevail in the advertising directed to specific industries in their respective trade publications.

In addition to preparing and placing advertising, the promotion director, working with a team of writers and artists, and drawing on the research department for statistical information and analytical help, will also develop presentations of both general and specific nature, create and execute direct mail campaigns, consult with sales and general management where necessary, and, in general, see to the promotional needs of the sales staff at large.

CLASSIFIED ADVERTISING

Classified advertising, or "want ads" as they used to be called, is a very important function in the newspaper advertising sales operation. The classified advertising manager usually directs a large staff including street sales people and phone operators. The classified pages are broken down in various categories sometimes numbering over 100. Many newspapers have gone out of their way to make the pages more attractive and legible.

According to Ms. Cal Tremblay, vice-president of Harte-Hanks Communications, and corporate director of classified advertising for the company, "Classified advertising is the real strength of the newspaper industry. Not only is it a tremendous revenue producer, but it also creates readership greater than that found in our editorial columns. The success of classified is normally a leading indicator of the overall success of the entire operation of a newspaper."[3]

It is sometimes the little things that help make big newspaper advertising sales. Every so often it is probably a good thing to indulge in a little self-analysis of our selling techniques. Sometimes it may give us a jolt to discover that we've been neglecting some of the basics in this business of newspaper space selling.

It is just as easy to get careless about some of the fine points in the technique of successful newspaper advertising space selling as it is to forget the components of a good golf swing or tennis stroke.

Following are the author's "seventeen timely tips" for selling newspaper advertising:

1. *Sell from top to bottom.* Don't overlook the person who is on the way up; one day he or she may be at the top. While the top executives must be covered, don't neglect the second – and even third – stringers. They are excellent sources of information, and when they move to the top, they will be our loyal friends.

2. *Make sure there is a steady flow of promotion material to agencies and clients.* It is important that all pertinent promotion material on your newspaper is readily available and, wherever possible, in the files of advertising decision makers. If they don't have a file already, try to get them to start one – and then keep it "alive."

3. *Review regularly your overall newspaper story with media buying executives.* Never take it for granted that the buyer is familiar with your story. There is no "best time" to bring the buyer up to date. Don't take it for granted when you are carrying the business that everything is

all right. Running accounts are your most important list of prospects. Regular advertisers are also the most vulnerable to the attacks of competitive media.

4. *Follow through between calls with intelligent sales letters.* "Out of sight, out of mind." The newspaper that comes first to the buyer's mind is the newspaper that is constantly and effectively sold. Good follow-up letters are often as important as in-person contacts and are essential in achieving adequate coverage.

5. *Review the contents of your briefcase at least once a month.* Your newspaper spends a lot of money on fact sheets and marketing data for your use. Make sure on your calls that you have every competitive advantage in your favor by keeping your material completely up to date. This should start with several representative copies of the newspaper and its features.

6. *Use everyone and anyone who can help you make the sale. Everyone at your newspaper is part of your sales team.* If you sense a cooling off on the part of a key advertising contact, if the person is harder to see than formerly, it's probably a good sign that you are losing ground. Don't keep these danger signs to yourself – run scared. Talk it over with the rest of the staff and management. From top to bottom every single member of your organization should be ready to help you make the sale, either with the advertiser or from behind the scenes.

7. *Organize your time efficiently for better coverage.* Try to make every hour a productive one. Plan your calls and try to make as many appointments as possible with key people. Organization of your time is especially important on extended trips from city to city where advanced planning is essential to get the most out of each day.

8. *Reader interest can be your most powerful selling tool.* When you call on an advertiser or agency executive, always have something with you that indicates the powerful readership appeal of your newspaper. Reader interest is the most undersold sales asset a newspaper has. And remember, a person's memory is short-lived. Tomorrow they'll forget your newspaper's editorial appeal of yesterday. Keep them posted editorially.

9. *Sell the decision makers.* An important newspaper buy can be costly; for many advertisers it's their most expensive buy. Final decisions for such expenditures are not left to space buyers alone. Surround your accounts both in the agency and at the client level.

10. *Sell a plan, not a page!* Your newspaper has many strong selling points. They are often not easy to interpret. It is big – it has tremendous

power – and it has deep penetration of your market. All the more reason for going in with a selling plan outlining a schedule – fitting in other media and placing an entire newspaper development program behind the drive.

11. *Have a good "opener" for your presentation.* If you get the agency executive or client on your side in the first 20 seconds, the chances of their staying with you all the way are good. Good salespeople spend as much time on a good lead into their pitch as they do on the rest of the subject matter itself. Try to figure out an approach that will get the buyer agreeing with you from the beginning. Get their full attention in that make-or-break first 20 seconds.

12. Visual presentations are aids, not crutches! Visual aids are often valuable for large groups and for certain types of subject matter. They are also effective in across-the-desk selling. But don't depend on them to do all the work for you. You are the expert. Project your own personality and knowledge into the presentation. A presentation never closed a sale; at best, it's a means to an end. Remember, some of the most successful sales aids have been scribbled – but significant – notes on a scrap of paper.

13. *Constantly work on improving your group presentation techniques.* Are you speaking to the audience or at them? Are your voice, facial expression, and demeanor pleasant? Try to put sincerity into your sales points. Bring your audience into the act by referring to people and accounts by name. Finish your sentences. Make your point and stop.

14. *Develop a sense of confidence.* Know you are going to make the sale before you make the call. Confidence should not be confused with cockiness. Be self-assured in a reserved manner.

15. *Be prepared.* Nothing is more important than proper and thorough preparation before making a newspaper sales call. Study the problems of your accounts, their objectives and marketing strategies.

16. *Don't be a one-account salesperson.* Too many newspaper salespeople concentrate on one or two favorite accounts because of personal contacts or familiarity. This results in serious neglect of other accounts.

17. *Understand your newspaper's research.* Your newspaper sales proposals must be backed up by research data. In order for a salesperson to present research, a most important sales tool, in an intelligent manner, one must study the technique, methodology, and results of both your own and your competition's research.

RESEARCH

Research, in one form or another, plays a significant role in the sale of newspaper advertising space. In the competitive marketplace in which newspapers exist, advertisers and agencies are in continual need of information on which they can make better media-buying decisions and of help in finding answers to such marketing problems as identifying and reaching their target markets or determining buyer motivation and buying patterns. The job of the research director is to develop and convey such information and help, with due regard for the newspaper's own sales objectives.

Research, then, embraces two disciplines: media research and market research, although some feel the latter function should be defined as advertising research. The *media research manager* is responsible for the statistical and analytical phases of newspaper research. These areas involve the understanding, interpretation, and projection of figures derived from various audience studies which the advertising industry usually accepts as impartial sources of newspaper audience numbers, demographics, and product purchase and ownership patterns. Other sources define, quantify, and report the psychographic characteristics of people in terms of their life-style patterns, which media researchers relate to the demographic profiles of their newspaper's audience, to establish their values as potential customers for the advertiser's products.

The *market research manager's* efforts are concentrated mainly in product areas, where studies of buying attitudes, motivations, perceptions, and habits are conducted on behalf of specific industries. While sophisticated advertisers may have voluminous research of their own, it is usually of a proprietary nature, and, thus, unavailable on an industrywide basis. A newspaper's market research may help confirm those advertisers' own findings while, at the same time, providing needed information for those lacking the facilities or the budget to do their own research. Some media research includes information on the relative values of competing media, a factor that supports the claim of those who believe that the exercise should, in fact, be called advertising research.

An excellent example of a most professional presentation based on reader and market research is the Phoenix Newspapers annual "Inside Phoenix" presentation which is shown each March in Symphony Hall in Phoenix Civic Plaza and is also published in book form. This presentation and study are both under the direction of Conrad A. Kloh, director of sales and marketing, and Ellen Baar Jacobs, market research manager.

NOTES

1. Raymond McKinney, *Selling Retail Advertising* (Albany, NY: The Press Company, Inc., 1944), foreword.

2. Personal Interview with Vance Stickell, executive vice president, Marketing the *Los Angeles Times,* Los Angeles, CA, March 6, 1984.

3. D. Earl Newsom, *The Newspaper* (Englewood Cliffs, NJ: Prentice-Hall, Inc., 1981), p. 133.

5 ———————————————

AMERICAN NEWSPAPER PUBLISHERS ASSOCIATION

Amendment I
Congress shall make no law respecting an establishment of religion, or prohibiting the free exercise thereof; or abridging the freedom of speech, or of the press; or the right of the people peaceably to assemble, and to petition the government for a redress of grievances.

The American Newspaper Publishers Association (ANPA) is a trade association of 1,384 member newspapers, mostly U.S. dailies, although membership includes non-dailies and newspapers published in Canada and elsewhere in the Western Hemisphere. ANPA member newspapers account for more than 90 percent of U.S. daily circulation, and 85 percent of the daily circulation in Canada.

ANPA was founded in 1887 at Rochester, NY. Charter members came from 12 states in the East and Midwest. An office was established in New York City where ANPA maintained headquarters until it moved to its Newspaper Center building in Reston, VA, near Washington, D.C., in 1972.

ANPA maintains close, cooperative relationships with other newspaper and journalism organizations. Located at the Newspaper Center in Reston are offices of:

ANPA
ANPA Foundation
ANPA Credit Bureau Inc.

American Society of Newspaper Editors
International Circulation Managers Association
International Newspaper Promotion Association
Newspaper Personnel Relations Association
Nihon Shinbun Kyokai (Japan Newspaper Publishers and Editors Association)
World Press Freedom Committee
Society of Newspaper Design

ANPA is a member of the International Federation of Newspaper Publishers (FIEJ), the World Press Freedom Committee, and the International Press Telecommunications Council.

ANPA serves the varied needs of its member newspapers through a number of departments:

Membership. Maintains close contact with member newspapers, assuring that various ANPA services are channeled to executives according to each member's needs; develops cost-effective programs to encourage membership, including ANPASURE custom insurance program and discount agreements for rental or lease of motor vehicles.

Industry and Public Affairs. Monitors readership and circulation matters; coordinates ANPA liaison with other newspaper business associations; performs publications policy review and edits all publications, except *Presstime*; handles press and public relations for the Association; responds to inquiries of member newspapers, the press, and the public.

Newsprint. Assists member newspapers with transportation details of shipments; training programs; sponsors an annual conference for newspaper trainers.

Legal. Represents the interests of newspapers before the courts and the regulatory agencies of government; provides member newspapers with information on legal matters affecting newspaper operations.

Government. Monitors and reports to member newspapers and the Association on government matters including free press, business, telecommunications, workplace and employee relations, taxes, and postal, advertising, and international matters; represents the interests of the newspaper business in its dealings with all branches of government at all levels, both domestic and international.

Telecommunications. Tracks new technology developments, analyzes telecommunications industry trends, and identifies new business opportunities.

ANPA News Research Center. At Syracuse University, NY, conducts research to help newspapers improve their editorial product. Research findings are published in ANPA News Research Reports.

Presstime. Monthly journal of ANPA, covering all aspects of the newspaper business, including news-editorial, news research, readership, circulation, advertising, marketing-promotion, employee relations, training, newsprint, technology and telecommunications; reports on governmental, postal, international and educational matters; includes in-depth analyses of current issues and trends in the newspaper business; keeps member newspapers abreast of the activities of the Association.[1]

The two major annual meetings sponsored by ANPA offer newspaper executives the opportunity to meet with colleagues from the newspaper business and related industries. The annual ANPA convention includes the Association's annual business meeting and features a three-day program of speakers, panels, and discussion sessions on matters of interest and importance to the newspaper business.

ANPA Convention
1984 – Montreal, April 30-May 2
1985 – Miami Beach, May 6-8

Daily Newspaper Circulation
(U.S. morning, evening, and Sunday circulation, 1946-1984)

Year	Morning	Evening	Total (M & E)	Sunday
1946	20,545,908	30,381,597	50,927,505	43,665,364
1950	21,266,126	32,562,946	53,829,072	46,582,348
1955	22,183,408	33,963,951	56,147,359	46,447,658
1960	24,028,788	34,852,958	58,881,746	47,698,651
1965	24,106,776	36,250,787	60,357,563	48,600,090
1970	25,933,783	36,173,744	62,107,527	49,216,602
1975	25,490,186	36,165,245	61,655,431	51,096,393
1980	29,414,036	32,787,804	62,201,840	54,671,755
1981	30,552,316	30,878,429	61,430,745	55,180,004
1982	33,174,087	29,313,090	62,487,177	56,260,764
1983[a]	33,570,242	29,041,494	62,611,741	56,714,895
1984[b]	35,682,998	27,657,338	63,340,336	57,511,975

[a]Revised figures.
[b]Preliminary figures.

Source: ANPA, *Editor & Publisher.*

Single-Copy Sales Price
(U.S. daily and Sunday newspapers*, 1965-1984)

Daily

Year	5¢	10¢	15¢	20¢	25¢	30¢	35¢	40¢	50¢
1965	456	892	3	2	–	–	–	–	–
1970	46	1,507	139	5	1	–	–	–	–
1975	4	428	1,153	137	10	1	–	–	–
1980	–	41	497	644	555	9	7	1	–
1981	–	30	290	437	960	17	15	1	–
1982	–	14	143	272	1,227	29	16	3	–
1983	–	10	91	183	1,306	80	24	3	–
1984	–	6	61	111	1,316	109	75	2	2

Sunday

Year	5¢	10¢	15¢	20¢	25¢	30¢	35¢	40¢	45¢	50¢
1965	21	128	190	143	45	5	–	–	–	–
1970	2	89	115	140	161	30	35	3	–	4
1975	–	37	61	49	170	58	157	37	3	51
1980	–	5	50	25	84	29	121	30	6	291
1981	–	–	33	16	77	24	88	21	3	313
1982	–	–	21	17	77	14	61	17	1	326
1983	–	–	5	12	88	8	44	15	3	309
1984	–	–	3	8	83	6	31	6	0	301

Year	55¢	60¢	65¢	70¢	75¢	80¢	85¢	90¢	95¢	$1.00
1965	–	–	–	–	–	–	–	–	–	–
1970	–	–	–	–	–	–	–	–	–	–
1975	1	4	–	–	1	–	–	–	–	–
1980	–	23	5	1	46	–	1	2	–	1
1981	4	22	2	–	117	–	3	–	–	5
1982	1	23	6	1	160	1	5	2	1	15
1983	1	26	5	1	170	1	6	3	–	60
1984	1	19	2	1	219	3	8	2	–	82

*These tables reflect daily and Sunday newspaper single-copy sales prices in five-cent increments to illustrate a trend. Newspapers selling for odd cents have been omitted, as have specialized newspapers.

Source: ANPA.

Daily Newspaper Advertising Volume

Year	National Advertising (millions)	Local Advertising (millions)	Total Newspaper Advertising (millions)	Index	Gross National Product[a] (billions)	Index
1946	$ 238	$ 917	$ 1,155	100.0	$ 208.5	100.0
1950	518	1,552	2,070	179.2	284.8	136.6
1955	712	2,365	3,077	266.4	398.0	190.9
1960	778	2,903	3,681	318.7	503.7	241.6
1965	784	3,642	4,426	383.2	684.9	328.5
1970	891	4,813	5,704	493.9	977.1	468.6
1975[a]	1,109	7,125	8,234	712.9	1,516.3	727.2
1980[a]	1,963	12,831	14,794	1,280.8	2,626.1	1,259.5
1981	2,259	14,269	16,528	1,430.9	2,937.7	1,408.9
1982	2,452	15,242	17,694	1,531.9	3,073.0	1,473.8
1983[a]	2,734	17,848	20,582	1,781.9	3,310.8	1,587.9
1984[b]	3,005	20,830	23,835	2,063.6	3,664.2	1,757.4

[a]Revised figures.
[b]Preliminary estimates.
Source: ANPA, U.S. Department of Commerce; McCann-Erickson Inc.

1986 – San Francisco, April 21-23
1987 – New York City, May 4-6
1988 – Honolulu, April 25-27
1989 – Chicago, April 24-26

The annual ANPA Operations Management Conference and Exposition (formerly the Production Management Conference) combines five days of the largest annual trade show of newspaper systems and equipment with a conference program of speakers, panel discussions, and demonstrations of equipment designed to help improve newspaper production operations. The influence and effect of future technology is featured.

ANPA Operations Management Conference and Exposition
1984 – Atlanta, June 9-13
1985 – New Orleans, June 8-12
1986 – Atlanta, June 21-25

1987 – Las Vegas, June 6-10
1988 – Atlanta, June 11-15
1989 – New Orleans, June 10-14

The ANPA Credit Bureau Incorporated (ANPA/CBI), a wholly owned subsidiary of the American Newspaper Publishers Association, has been helping newspapers manage credit problems for more than 90 years. ANPA/CBI is not merely a collection service; its staff consists of media credit specialists with expertise and information that no other company possesses. Credit Bureau files contain information on more than half a million national, regional, and local advertisers, mass marketers, ad agencies, and others. And its automated facilities help improve profits and eliminate wasted time.

ANPA/CBI operates like an association, allowing subscribers to share information that concerns all media.

As specialists in media credit, ANPA/CBI personnel are on top of developments affecting media credit.

ANPA/CBI services are flexible, so subscribers can purchase only those service elements that are necessary. Whether only one person handles everything from bookkeeping to bill collection, or your operation has a full-scope credit department, ANPA/CBI can function as your department.

Creative research and development programs have transformed the newspaper publishing business from inefficient, manual, hot-lead processes to ultra-high-speed, automated and electronic systems for editing, printing, and packaging today's product. The ANPA Research Center is recognized as a leader in the development of many of these new systems.

The Center operates in several ways to improve newspaper production by developing and testing new equipment and techniques and by investigating promising concepts for future technology.

Member newspapers can call on trained professionals for consultation services to help solve equipment and operating problems, including installation and evaluation of new equipment and correction of print quality or equipment malfunctions.

Creative research and development programs have transformed the newspaper publishing business from inefficient, manual, hot-lead processes to ultra-high-speed, automated and electronic systems for editing, printing, and packaging today's product. The ANPA Research Center is recognized as a leader in the development of many of these new systems.

The Center operates in several ways to improve newspaper production by developing and testing new equipment and techniques and by investigating promising concepts for future technology.

Member newspapers can call on trained professionals for consultation services to help solve equipment and operating problems, including installation and evaluation of new equipment and correction of print quality or equipment malfunctions.

ANPA's technical experts also provide testing services for the analysis of inks and newsprint and establish color standards used by all ink manufacturers. The Computer Applications Section develops practical software programs useful for newspaper operations.

ANPA's catalytic research efforts, carried out in cooperation with manufacturers and suppliers, focus on future technology and at the same time strive to improve existing systems and procedures in areas such as smaller, lightweight printing presses; non-petroleum-based inks; inking systems and substitute newsprint fibers.[2]

INTERNATIONAL NEWSPAPER ADVERTISING AND MARKETING EXECUTIVES ASSOCIATION

This association is better known by its initials, INAME. It is an association made up of newspaper advertising and marketing executives in this country and overseas.

The objects for which it was formed are to further the understanding and use of advertising in daily newspapers; to provide means of contact between its members represented by newspaper advertising and marketing executives, business and general managers, publishers and newspaper representatives of daily newspapers; to consider ways and means tending to increase efficiency and economy in the production of newspaper advertising and its marketing in daily newspapers; to promote the closer relationship and consequent better understanding between the buyers of advertising, their agents, and the daily newspaper.[3]

In an interview, Sidney W. Bordelon, general manager and secretary-treasurer of the organization, described the association as follows:

"Getting things done and/or making things happen" is what INAME and its membership is about! You know we don't sell newspaper advertising . . . that's the Newspaper Advertising Bureau's job. Nor are we promotion experts or circulation wizards . . . but advertising-marketing is utterly dependent on them plus editorial to be able to go out into the ever-changing marketplace to fill our pages with result-getting advertisements.

That newspaper advertising revenues will top 23-odd billion dollars in 1984 doesn't necessarily mean we are crackerjacks at selling our customers. On the contrary, newspapers' share of the total advertising dollar seems to continue to shrink to about 27 percent while there are untold millions of dollars in national/general advertising that we cannot reach. That circulation has hovered around 63 million for the last several years still means we aren't giving our customers the content or quality of editorial-advertising nor capturing the ever-expanding readership potential. Despite our years of efforts somebody else is out there working even harder and is more productive in satisfying customer demands than we are.

So we're holding our own and with the tremendous technological advances over the last 15 years we have reached probably the most important plateau of all . . . and that is the self-awareness that even though newspapers are the only true mass medium . . . they have taken their audiences for granted for too long and underestimated the skills of their competitors so we have found ourselves in the unenviable position of playing catch-up. And that doesn't happen overnight!

So what is INAME doing about all of this to help our membership? Well here goes: Our two (January and July) annual sales conferences are better attended and highly programmed to address the challenges of . . . devising Standard Advertising Units, producing better color, upgrading staff sales skills, increasing managerial proficiency and techniques, generating new sales/revenue producing ideas for the membership and helping our members counter the competition which is attacking newspapers' share of the market from all directions.

As one president after another has said, "Perk, the backbone of the Association is its committees!" The ANPA/Liaison Format, chaired by Frank Savino of the Hackensack, New Jersey Bergen County Record, is a new committee. He and the ANPA Working Committee have given several years of their time and energies to bringing about the Standard Advertising Unit system adoption due to take effect July 1, 1984. But we're sure you are already knowledgeable on this subject. Just wanted to point out that our Chairpeople do yeomen service to the Association and are truly the ones who "make it happen . . . get things done!"

Another example of this motto, if you will, is Robert Cutler's production of the booklet "Newspapers: The Effective Medium." We made this available to all members at no charge and it was simply a compilation of some of the Newspaper Advertising Bureau's standard slides compiled in an easy to understand and presentation format. But his ingenuity benefited all of our more than 1,000 newspapers!

Incidentally, Robert, who is Advertising Director of *The Salt Lake Tribune,* has been the chairman of our Schools & Colleges Committee for about six years now and under his leadership we established the INAME Foundation in 1979. With a meager $60,000 in contributions the Foundation has managed to conduct four annual Educator Seminars in New York City (all expenses paid), fund numerous Newspaper Advertising Bureau projects to over 125 colleges and universities at no charge (including several Creative Newspaper projects) and produce a newspaper course outline (which we're sure you have received) as well as the most recent project . . . a booklet on business side internships. For Bob it has truly been an unceasing labor of love and we are delighted to let you know that within the next few months the Foundation will be conducting a campaign to secure a $1,000,000 fund . . . and the interest from that endowment is expected to yield about $100,000 annually . . . and all of this will go directly toward benefiting the professors and students at our journalism/communications schools and colleges! Its specific goals have been identified . . . but not yet approved, so it's a bit premature to say what the funds will be used for at this time. But we can tell you that it will be the most ambitious undertaking newspaper advertising has ever conducted . . . and we expect its impact to endure for many years to come.

Well, Perk, that will really wrap up our contributions to you. I could have gone on and on, but realize you have been exposed to a lot of the materials we've produced over the years . . . so may we just leave it with "if any of this material needs further elaboration and/or you decide we have inadvertently created some gaps" . . . then please don't hesitate to let us know, we'll do our very best to supplement.

Finally, thanks for your indulgence and giving us the opportunity to make a contribution. We know your book will be a most successful one.[4]

Organization

INAME is a non-profit group of advertising directors and managers, and marketing/business and sales executives of daily newspapers in the United States, Canada, and several foreign countries. It was founded in

1911 and today represents approximately 90 percent of the daily newspaper circulation in North America with more than 3,000 members from over 1,000 papers. Newspapers of all sizes share similar problems and meet on common ground in INAME. Members range in size from less than 5,000 circulation to more than 1,000,000. Sixty percent of the member papers, however, are under 30,000 circulation. Membership is in the name of the firm, which designates an executive to exercise the active membership and voting rights. Up to three associate executives can also be listed in the roster at no added dues charge.[5]

Goals

The objectives of INAME are varied. It strives to: further the understanding and use of advertising in daily newspapers; provide means of contact between its members represented by daily newspaper advertising executives, business managers, publishers, and newspaper representatives; consider ways and means to increase efficiency and economy in the production of daily newspaper addvertising; and promote the closer relationship and better understanding between the buyer of advertising, his agent, and the newspaper.[6]

Sales Conferences

Members reap the benefits of membership through two yearly sales conferences each January and July. These meetings are regionalized so all members can attend regularly. Many outstanding and diversified speakers address these gatherings. Members have major roles in these conferences through participation in Ideas Tables – small groups of advertising executives that meet to discuss management problems and successes of the business. Most members constantly turn the information obtained from an Ideas table session into advertising revenue.

These conferences also offer the world's largest tearsheet exhibit of innovative and adaptable newspaper advertising collected from hundreds of member papers.[7]

Benefits

From INAME's many active committees have come valuable selling tools and sales training aids. In addition to the association's informative monthly *NEWS*, which helps keep newspapers abreast of the latest developments in newspaper advertising, there is the *Sales & Idea* book. This is a collection of 100 outstanding ads from the semiannual Sales Conference Exhibits. It's a reservoir of saleable, adaptable ads. In addition, a membership in INAME affords the opportunity of using the many sales training courses and materials developed specifically for newspaper advertising sales by the INAME Sales Training Committee. These include:

"Retail Marketing." This popular marketing workbook for newspaper sales professionals is the newest training program available to INAME members. It gives newspaper sales pros practical insight on how retailers think and operate and it identifies ways to become more effective with all your retail advertising accounts. This is the only course available anywhere written for newspaper ad staffs dealing with retail marketing.

"Positive Selling." The successful sales training program with 14 chapters of solid, practical sales ideas and approaches.

"Copy & Layout." Improves newspaper staff's creativity in all areas of writing strong copy and effective layout. This course/workshop comes complete with cassette, slides and presenter's manual.[8]

"Prepare Like A PRO." A 16-mm film dealing exclusively with newspaper advertising sales. This realistic, true-to-life presentation offers thought provoking ideas on making calls, giving presentations, and handling objections. A contemporary approach that today's sales people can relate to.[9]

Following are INAME's active committees reaching into all facets of the newspaper advertising business: ABC Liaison, Advertising Agency Relations, Advertising Council, Advertising Measurements, ANPA Liaison, Classified Advertising, Color Advertising, Co-op Advertising, Exhibits, General Advertising Sales, Legislative Information, Marketing, Membership, Movie, National Advertiser Relations, New Technology, Research, Retail Advertiser Relations, Sales Training, Schools & Colleges, Small Newspapers, and Telecommunications.[10]

All too often, the typical college advertising student sets his or her sights first on the large agency as a career goal – a place where fame is derived from creating "where's the beef?" blockbusters. A creative, top agency job is where the action is, he or she may think.

But sometime during the senior year, reality comes into focus: top agency creative departments normally don't hire recent graduates. When this student realizes "a need to continue eating after graduation day," as one professor told us this past month, he or she will consider a career near the bottom of the list of possibilities: one in newspaper advertising.

Unfortunately, as those of us in the business know, the student is underestimating the newspaper's possibilities. Not only would a newspaper career offer creative challenges, but the business also is actively seeking to attract more recent graduates into its ranks.

Necessary to that recruitment effort is the enhancement of the newspaper's business-side image.[11]

NOTES

1.   "Facts About Newspapers," Public Affairs Department, American Newspaper Publishers Association, April 1985.

2.   Source: ANPA.

3.   Bylaws of the INAME.

4.   Personal interview with Sidney W. Bordelon, general manager and secretary-treasurer of INAME, Reston, VA, May 11, 1984.

5.   INAME files.

6.   Ibid.

7.   Ibid.

8.   Ibid.

9.   Ibid.

10.   Ibid.

11.   *INAME NEWS*, April 1984, p. 2.

6

THE NEWSPAPER ADVERTISING BUREAU

> At a time when conventional wisdom calls for audience
> selectivity in the use of media, it is well to remember that the
> most crucial element of selectivity is exercised by consumers
> themselves. It occurs at the first level at which advertisements
> either mobilize their attention or are assimilated as background
> noise.[1]
>
> Dr. Leo Bogart

The Newspaper Advertising Bureau (NAB) is a non-profit sales, research, marketing, and promotion organization that has been helping member newspapers and the advertising community to use newspapers more effectively since 1913. Nearly 1,000 U.S. and Canadian newspapers are members of the Bureau. The home office is in New York and there are five regional offices. The Bureau has 158 people on staff. The Bureau is headed by the president, Craig C. Standen, and is governed by a board of directors and two plans committees, one for the United States and one for Canada. The board is made up of 49 publishers from newspapers of all sizes in all regions of the United States and Canada. The board and its chairman meet three times a year to discuss newspaper problems and opportunities and to guide the Bureau's course of strategy. The plans committees are composed of newspaper advertising directors who meet twice a year to discuss and implement sales projects, and to coordinate activities applicable to both countries.[2]

William A. Thomson was the first director of the then Bureau of Advertising in 1913 and held that post until 1948. He wrote an excellent book in 1952 outlining the history of the Bureau and some of the methods used in coping with serious problems during the Great Depression and the war years.[3]

National advertising volume continued to drop in 1932 as the depression deepened. The Bureau lost membership steadily as newspapers cut expenses. In April of that year, Edwin S. Friendly, of the *New York Sun,* succeeded W. E. Macfarlane as chairman of the Committee in Charge. Macfarlane received the thanks of the Committee in Charge for his devotion to the Bureau's interests, and agreed to continue on the committee and to serve as vice-chairman. There had been a number of additions to the Committee in Charge under Macfarlane, including W. A. Elliott (*Jacksonville* [FL] *Times-Union*); George Auer (*New York Herald Tribune*); Roy D. Moore (Brush-Moore Newspapers); and Fred Schilpliu (*St. Cloud* [MN] *Times-Journal*). Frank G. Huntress (*San Antonio Express and Evening News*) joined the committee soon after Friendly became chairman, and the following April, James G. Stahlman (*Nashville Banner*), was appointed a member. Elmer DeClerque, Sylvester Blish, and John T. Fitzgerald, representatives from Chicago, served as advisory members for the period.[4]

Both the ANPA and the Bureau thought it best to ride out the storm by slashing expenses as their members were doing. The first step, taken toward the close of 1932, was to reduce dues 10 percent and to cut all staff salaries above a nominal minimum. Within three months it was necessary to make a second cut of 10 percent in staff pay and to eliminate some personnel.[5]

Frank E. Tripp, of Gannett Newspapers, was an active member of the Newspaper Advertising Executives Association (NAEA) as well as a member of the Committee in Charge of the Bureau of Advertising. He made a speech at the October 17, 1935 meeting of the NAEA in Chicago and started a chain of events that led eventually to the establishment of the Bureau on the solid footing it enjoys today.

Tripp voiced in his speech a complaint that was fairly general in the newspaper business that there was something radically lacking in the newspapers' effort to sell their medium. He asserted that not more than $125,000 was being spent on general newspaper advertising promotion by the Bureau of Advertising and by Major Market Newspapers, Inc. This, he said, was a puny fraction of 1 percent of the $163 million of national advertising carried in 1934 by newspapers, and obviously was one of the reasons advertising agencies and advertisers were turning from newspapers. Another reason was that newspapers spent their time fighting one another instead of cooperating to create new business and standing up to their competition from magazines and radio. He called for a "united front" and thus named the movement that was to follow.[6]

The Committee in Charge met two days later in Chicago and Tripp reported his speech and the discussion that followed it. He said criticism of the Bureau by NAEA members had been general and at times bitter but that, sifted out, the Bureau was blamed more often for having too little money rather than for what it was trying to do with what it had. The upshot, he said, was the passage by the NAEA meeting of a resolution to appoint a committee that would look into ways and means of raising at least twice the budget the Bureau had and "to report on whether or not any existing organization was equipped to handle this expenditure for promotion or whether or not it was advisable to create a new organization for that purpose." Tripp was made chairman of this committee, which consisted of Leroy W. Herron, Fred G. Pearce, Herbert S. Conlon, Chesser M. Campbell, John Irwin, Thomas G. Murphy, and Don U. Bridge.[7]

COMMITTEE IS PROFOUNDLY IMPRESSED

The Committee in Charge passed a resolution saying "it was profoundly impressed" with the action of the NAEA and requested the Chair to appoint a subcommittee of three "to discuss the expenditure of a larger sum than the Bureau now has and to receive suggestions as to means of raising a larger fund." This passage, taken from the minutes of the session, was followed by another asserting that the Bureau was the logical organization to continue the promotion of newspapers as a medium and that all efforts at broadening this work should center in the present organization. The committee also passed a unanimous resolution of confidence in the director and his staff.[8]

The mission of the Newspaper Advertising Bureau is to help increase the revenues of the daily newspaper in the United States and Canada. The Bureau's primary job is to sell and promote the daily newspaper as an advertising medium. In addition, the Bureau undertakes related projects that will enhance the newspaper business over the long term.

Operationally, the Newspaper Advertising Bureau fulfills the following functions:

Sells and promotes the daily newspaper medium to top-level marketing and media decision makers responsible for national or regional business.

Supports the sales efforts of individual newspapers by providing marketing and media data, customized research results, professional training programs, and creative selling aids.

Serves as a marketing and media consultant to the daily newspaper business as well as to individual newspapers.

Develops and operates new marketing and media services that can improve newspaper selling efforts.

Undertakes special projects that will improve the long-term revenue potential for newspapers in areas such as circulation, readership, standardized ad formats, and satellite transmission.

Assumes a leadership role for the daily newspaper business by identifying problems and opportunities, and then developing appropriate plans to address them.

Serves as a communication center to ensure that all member newspapers are kept abreast of trends, opportunities, programs, and progress.[9]

NATIONAL ADVERTISING SALES

The National Advertising Sales Department, headed by Mac G. Morris, vice-president, takes the case for newspapers to the top with a regular program of calls on decision makers at the headquarters of major advertisers and their agencies. At the same time the Bureau produces a variety of materials: slide presentations, booklets, flow charts, and cassettes to promote the daily and Sunday newspaper as a productive sales medium.[10]

Increasing newspapers' share of total national dollars and selling continuity schedules are the prime functions of the National Sales Department. To this end, customized presentations are targeted to specific accounts and product categories. For example, "How to Win Votes and Influence People" spotlights the daily newspaper as the ideal medium for political advertising in national, state, and local elections. "Corporate and Advocacy Advertising in Newspapers" responds to the increasing importance of corporate, institutional, and public issue/advocacy advertising among major corporations, explaining how the daily newspaper provides a vital showcase for these two exploding types of advertising. This presentation has been shown to over 200 corporations and advertising agencies.[11]

Arming the newspaper business for the intermedia battle are three presentations, "An Evening with TV," "Reconsidering TV," and "The Measure of a Medium," which underscore the strengths of newspapers versus competitive media.

This department is also focused on the huge revenue potential generated by those companies created by the divestiture of AT&T. These firms, when taken as a whole, are expected to exceed any other national advertiser, and the NAB is working to ensure that newspapers get their share.[12]

The government deregulation of the financial business has opened a wide variety of revenue-generating services for the nation's banks, savings and loans, and brokerage firms to offer customers. The advertising dollars budgeted to these new areas are the target of a specially prepared financial presentation which shows each type of financial institution how they can get the most from their newspaper advertising dollars.[13]

Economical, long-range ad scheduling in daily newspapers is encouraged through the use of NEWSPLAN, the newspaper business' program of discounts for continuity that has been responsible for major breakthroughs and increased expenditures in newspapers by many large national advertisers. Over 1,000 newspapers and more than 130 advertisers have taken advantage of this unique opportunity to maximize the cost-effectiveness of their newspaper advertising.[14]

As part of its ongoing communications strategy, the National Sales Department regularly conducts in-house seminars for advertising agencies and for their clients. The aim is twofold: to introduce the newspaper business to those who are new to marketing and advertising, and to update seasoned pros on what's new in newspapers.[15]

RETAIL MARKETING DEPARTMENT

Retail advertising decisions are moving from local stores to headquarters. The Retail Marketing Department goes where the choices are made, selling the newspaper's strengths to national and regional retailers through systematic calls to top retail advertising decision makers and contacting retailers in all types of stores, from fashion to hardware, music to paints. The department also works closely with traditional department stores, mass merchandise companies, shopping centers, service firms, and specialty firms.[16]

In response to newspaper requests for background data on the total scope of the retail industry, the PARR system is used to appraise sales opportunities in local markets, zip code data are provided and analyzed, and marketing data drawn from retail seminars are disseminated and interpreted for member newspapers.[17]

The Retail Marketing Department, led by Alfred Eisenpreis, a vice president, is also recognized as an authoritative source for marketing data and trend evaluation of all aspects of the distribution field by agencies, manufacturers, academicians, and trade publications. Retail seminars bring the Bureau's newspaper advertising message to top management at major department stores and specialty store organizations. Three thousand retailers participated in one recent seminar series for Florida merchants.[18]

Many presentations also are customized for and targeted to individual companies after an analysis of their particular needs. Recommendations are made in cooperation with newspaper advertising directors for the markets involved.[19]

The Retail Marketing Department provides timely sales aids suited to newspapers of all sizes in the United States and Canada. Recent projects include "Profitability Profiles for Shopping Centers," "The Paper Clip Test for Retail Newspaper Advertising," "Is There a Doctor in the House?" (a check-up and check-list for healthy stores), and the NAB-NRMA presentation, "The One-Day Only, Final Clearance, All-Sizes, Half-Price, Pre-Holiday, Famous Retailers' Sale Advertising in Newspapers Show," whose title speaks for itself.

The Bureau also conducts citywide retail seminars in over 30 cities a year, reaching more than 5,000 retail ad executives with programs that help them make their newspaper advertising investment more effective.[20]

FOOD STORE SALES

To help newspapers increase their revenues from both retail and national food advertisers, the NAB's Food Division headed by Richard Neale, a vice president, runs a regular program of newspaper support and personal industry contacts among leading chains, major manufacturers and brokers, and industry associations.[21]

Support information for newspapers includes:

1. The "Food Ad Bulletin," spotlighting advertising success stories.
2. The "National Product Movement Report," based on scanner data, showing increases in sales of items that have been advertised in newspapers.
3. Retail product movement scanner data showing similar results from retail newspaper ads.
4. An annual report on food retailing advertising plans and practices, entitled "Current Trends in Food Marketing."
5. New research on such subjects as "The Emerging New Food Shopper" and "Food Shopping in a One-Person Household."[22]

CO-OP DEPARTMENT

Co-op is a proven profit source for newspapers. Current estimates put the amount of co-op funds available for advertising at close to $8 billion annually. But approximately 40 percent goes unused.[23]

To capture those co-op dollars for newspapers, the Bureau's Co-op Sales Department in Chicago provides a wealth of co-op sales tools, plus computer access to over 3,100 manufacturer co-op plans.

In addition, the Co-op Sales staff works continually to increase a newspaper's return on its co-op investment through hundreds of direct sales calls to manufacturers, major wholesalers, and retailers across the United States and Canada.[24]

Two complete co-op selling systems are available to Bureau members: RCR and NCN.

RCR (Retail Co-op Recovery) is a computer-assisted system designated for selling retail accounts. The RCR category printouts uncover available co-op accruals, while the Co-op Plan-o-Gram allocates these funds without complicated computation and allows a retailer's ad budget to be doubled at very little additional cost to the advertiser. The RCR worksheets simplify paperwork for both the retailer and the newspaper, and the RCR Claim Package insures prompt reimbursement and ready funds for continued newspaper advertising.[25]

NCN (Newspaper Co-op Network) provides manufacturers, distributors, and their agencies with a simple One Order/One Bill placement service for multiple dealer-listing co-op ads. Working with INAME and the Advertising Checking Bureau, NCN has placed millions of dollars of newspaper co-op ads, at no cost to individual newspapers.

On behalf of Bureau members a Co-op Audit Service for department stores and chain retailers is also available. The audit process identifies new co-op dollars, recommends directions for expansion, and institutes a co-op tracking system.[26]

CLASSIFIED DEPARTMENT

The Classified Department is working to maintain classified linage gains and build on them. The development of product managers who specialize in real estate, employment, automotive, and general merchandise markets has added strength to the classified selling effort.[27]

The major activities of the department are in research, training, workshops, sales tools, and promotion. Classified research is a continuing source of data for sales tools and materials. Training programs are continually developed for both telephone sales and outside salespeople.[28]

Strong links with industry associations and key advertiser groups in the real estate, automotive, and employment markets are maintained through major presentations, newsletters, and personal contact, as well as through participation in task force groups on major projects. For example, members of the department are active in newspaper groups that are working on the opportunities in classified that relate to the new information technologies.[29]

MARKETING-CREATIVE

The Bureau's staff of copywriters, art directors, and production experts produces sales materials for NAB sales and marketing people and for member newspapers to use in their own selling.[30]

Much effort goes into major multimedia presentations based on original research and marketing concepts. These presentations involve the use of state-of-the-art computer programmed systems to choreograph dozens of audio and visual sources. The presentations are usually premiered to advertising decision makers at major meetings like the National Retail Merchants Association's annual convention, then converted into single tray slide presentations for member use.[31]

Creative also turns out printed sales tools: desk-top easel presentations, booklets and brochures, the annual Planbooks, weekly newsletters, a monthly package of selling aids, and advertising campaigns for in-paper promotions. A major responsibility of the Creative Department is to help advertisers make better creative use of newspaper space. This is done by creating ads and campaign ideas for target advertisers, through articles and ad layouts in trade press articles, by sponsoring the annual Athena Awards honoring the year's best newspaper advertising, and by producing each year a Creative Newspaper and special slide presentation showcasing the Athena winners, advertisers who have made interesting and provocative use of the daily newspaper.[32]

RESEARCH

The Research Department has three principal functions: to provide support for the sales and marketing efforts of the NAB, to provide data and technical assistance for NAB service functions that include CAN DO and PARR, and to serve as an information source for newspaper advertisers, agencies, and member newspapers.

In order to achieve these objectives, the Research Department designs and carries out survey research involving readers, the newspaper, and products, and it does special analyses of economic and media data. For example, a large-scale Bureau study of ad readership showed that over 90 percent of the best prospects for an advertised product or store are interested in the advertisement for itself; in effect, newspaper ads "automatically" select their own best customers. This finding is consistent with earlier research.[33]

Sales tools can be based on nationally projectable studies documenting that the average page is opened by over three out of four of a newspaper's readers. Other recent studies cover aspects of the retail shopping experience. One shopping study reveals that among those who recall making unplanned purchases because of advertising, six of ten name the newspaper as the source of that advertising. The Research Department also coordinates research on newspaper editorial content and its applications to newspaper advertising.

The Media Information Services Center maintains records on advertising activity in all the media, with particular emphasis on newspapers. These records enable the Bureau to spot company and industry trends, sales opportunities, and potential trouble areas. Media Information Services also issues regular forecasts on the volume of newspaper advertising in broad categories during the year.[34]

The Bureau, in late 1984, moved to larger headquarters at 1180 Avenue of the Americas in New York City. The five regional offices, headed by regional vice-presidents, are located in Chicago, Detroit, Atlanta, Los Angeles, and San Francisco.

NOTES

1. Leo Bogart, executive vice-president, Newspaper Advertising Bureau, Inc., *Marketing and Media Decisions*, November 1983, p. 28.
2. Personal interview with Craig C. Standen, president, Newspaper Advertising Bureau, Inc., February 4, 1985, New York.
3. William A. Thomson, "High Adventure in Advertising," p. 109. New York: The North River Press, 1952.
4. Ibid.
5. Ibid.
6. Ibid., p. 114.
7. Ibid., p. 115.
8. Ibid.
9. Standen interview.
10. Personal interview with Mac G. Morris, National Sales, vice-president, Newspaper Advertising Bureau, Inc., February 4, 1985, New York.
11. Ibid.
12. Ibid.
13. Ibid.
14. Ibid.
15. Ibid.
16. Personal interview, Alfred Eisenpreis, vice-president, Retailing Marketing, Newspaper Advertising Bureau, Inc., February 4, 1985, New York.
17. Ibid.
18. Ibid.
19. Ibid.
20. Ibid.
21. Personal interview with Richard Neale, vice-president, Food Store Sales, Newspaper Advertising Bureau, Inc., February 4, 1985, New York.
22. Ibid.
23. Public Relations Department, Newspaper Advertising Bureau Bulletin, 1985.
24. Ibid.
25. Ibid.
26. Ibid.
27. Personal interview, William Solch, Classified Advertising Department, Newspaper Advertising Bureau, Inc., February 5, 1985, New York.
28. Ibid.
29. Ibid.
30. Personal interview, Henry A. Simons, vice-president, Creative director, Newspaper Advertising Bureau, Inc., February 5, 1985, New York.
31. Ibid.
32. Ibid.

33. Personal interview, Dr. Albert Gallin, vice-president, associate director of Research, Newspaper Advertising Bureau, Inc., February 5, 1985, New York.

34. Ibid.

7

NEW DEVELOPMENTS

> Reporting, inquiry, writing, editing, the principles of fair
> play and justice, the selection of news and how to place it in
> historical perspective . . . these are the fundamentals that must
> be taught, must be absorbed, must be practiced, if the free press is
> to play its role in our society – a role without which our society
> cannot function.[1]
>
> Walter Cronkite

A book on the practice of newspaper management would not be
complete without a chapter on the most interesting new developments in
the newspaper field.

USA TODAY

On August 27, 1982, the first president of the planned national
newspaper, *USA TODAY*, Phillip Giolanella and the editor, John Curley, wrote a letter to Gannett Company stockholders outlining their plans
for this new newspaper and setting a launching date of September 15,
1982.

This letter stated that Gannett had researched the project for three
years and reactions of newspaper readers and advertisers had been
overwhelmingly favorable. Their description of the unique publication
was outlined as follows:

> Because *USA TODAY*'s point of view isn't restricted to any one particular
> city, its journalistic "beat" ranges from Maine to Hawaii. So it's the one

paper, for example, that can help you spot a local fad before it becomes a coast-to-coast lifestyle; see how mob connections in New Jersey shape food prices in Iowa; and understand the national implications of a new source for home loans.[2]

The founder and guiding light behind this unique publication was the chairman and president of the Gannett Company, Allen H. Neuharth. In an interview published in *Marketing & Media Decisions*, Neuharth stated:

> We've made projections and set certain goals for each quarter and year. We have a five year plan and I think we can achieve success.
>
> News and information companies, by whatever means they have, must help people to learn more, learn to help each other more, and help people to grow. In our satellite society, people are continually on the move, have interests in other areas, have travelled, have their families and friends spread out. News and information companies can help us to become one nation. The more the media delivers this broader information package, the more the public gets and the more the public likes it. Some people say there is a glut of information out there. I don't agree. People want more information. That's why there is all news radio, why there is three hours of news a day on the TV networks.[3]

Besides *USA TODAY* the Gannett Company owns 87 daily newspapers in 34 states plus Guam and the Virgin Islands. Gannett is an imposing publishing enterprise with almost $2 billion in revenues and $223.9 million in profits in 1984. However, the attention has been focused on *USA TODAY*, and the publicity and promotion alone have been of staggering proportions.

This unique national newspaper started out, and has continued with, four main sections: Main News, Money, Sports, and Life. Time Inc. filed a suit against Gannett challenging the use of "Money" and "Life," which were identical to the logos of two of their prominent magazines. According to *Advertising Age* a settlement has been reached and it is believed the agreement stipulates *USA TODAY* can continue calling the two sections "Money" and "Life," but the section logos have been redesigned to minimize the resemblance to the Time Inc. trademarks.[4]

The circulation of *USA TODAY* has climbed steadily from the beginning. It has grown faster than any other newspaper in history. Its average daily net paid circulation increased as follows:

221,978	Oct. 1982
362,879	Nov. 1982
531,438	Jan. 1983
859,180	March 1983
1,151,416	Oct. 1983
1,239,887	Nov. 1983
1,328,781	Dec. 1983

Source: USA TODAY records according to estimates before official audit.

In March 1984, *Editor & Publisher* attempted to rate *USA TODAY* as an advertising medium, by interviewing four top advertising agency media executives. A summary of some of their comments from the interviews follows.

Kenneth E. Caffrey, senior vice-president and executive director of media operations, Ogilvy & Mather:

Some see *USA TODAY* as something between a newspaper and a magazine. Magazine advertisers will have to decide whether it offers advantages of topicality and immediacy not usually found in magazines. If they are newspaper advertisers, they may want to refocus their copy to take advantage of the unique environment. In either case, you will have a situation where special copy treatments may be indicated and advertisers will have to make individual decisions in dealing with that.

It is possible advertisers will rationalize the use of *USA TODAY* in one of two ways. First, as the newspaper for travelers. There are lots of travelers in the country and the business traveler has always been a highly desirable prospect for many advertisers. Second, as the supplementary buy in a market, *USA TODAY* could have meaning as the second newspaper in a market, especially when an advertiser wants to give an upscale lift to a campaign.

USA TODAY has been a great boon to the newspaper business generally. It has shaken many publishers from their stodgy dream world and got them thinking about making their properties more contemporary. Newspapers have encountered difficulties when they have been overtaken by change and ceased being relevant to their communities. Gannett has put a burr under the industry saddle and it's a healthy thing, for everyone.

Michael D. Drexler, executive vice-president/director of media and programming, Doyle, Dane, Bernbach Inc.:

It's been referred to as the newspaper of tomorrow, but that has to do with advances in color fidelity, graphics, computerized operations, and decentralized editing which allows editors in different parts of the country to contribute to the finished product. It does not mean the newspaper business of the future will become national. Newspapers will continue to thrive as a highly desirable local medium.

Gannett has packaged a superb product but they have yet to define its advertising particularity. Advertisers see it more as a magazine than a traditional newspaper and compare it with *Time, Newsweek,* and *U.S. News.* It's another kid on the block – not one on his own exclusive turf.

I'm glad to see they are testing higher cover prices. I have always felt they would eventually have to go as high as 50 cents to provide the income stream and cash flow that will enable them to turn out a quality product while lessening their dependence on the volatility of advertising budgets and scheduling.

A higher cover price is important too, because besides chains like Sears, K-Mart, and Penney along with some others, they are locked out of a lot of retail advertising which accounts for about 85 percent of all newspaper revenues.

For the year ahead we see happy days for newspapers generally. We predict revenues will reach $23.1 billion, a 13.6 percent increase over 1983. Circulation will continue its growth of the last several years. Local, retail, and classified advertising should increase about 14 percent for total revenues of $20.1 billion.

Michael Haggerty, vice-president and media director, New York Foote, Cone & Belding:

The question is asked as to the kind of audience *USA TODAY,* a national newspaper, can deliver. That implies specifically aiming at an identifiable audience whose members share common characteristics and interests.

I don't think a general newspaper can or should do that. I doubt if *USA TODAY* should constrict itself by appealing to a particular reader category.

As an ad buy I see it as delivering a mass audience, although not as mass as television but more selective, yet not as selective as special interest magazines. I think it is definitely a viable medium. We are always looking for broad coverage and it fits right in with that. And as it continues its rollout, its newspaper format, more advanced than any we've seen before, will become even more essential for advertisers.

It is hard for me at this moment to definitively rate *USA TODAY* as an ad medium. There are things that have to be appraised before I can determine that. Right now, I think it represents a good vehicle that will continue to build as their circulation increases.

We have used *USA TODAY* for some of our clients, but it would be difficult to measure the effectiveness of a single publication, especially when sales are up across the board for our clients generally.

Thurman R. Pierce, Jr., vice-president, U.S. Manager Print Media, J. Walter Thompson, USA, Inc.:

USA TODAY has succeeded in designing a successful editorial package targeted to professionals and a more affluent, predominantly male audience that travels a lot, spends more, and is influential in the business and professional communities.

It can, I believe, become an excellent medium for many advertisers who aim at this kind of audience. It has taken time for agencies to absorb this, but I believe in it; in the next few years *USA TODAY* will see their advertising increase, although not as fast as their readership. Even an excellent advertising package never gets advertisers as fast as readers – it's just a slower process.

Their research confirms they are reaching residents in "A" counties, the big markets, and that they are the high income readers we generally seek to attract via the newsweeklies. Inevitably, *USA TODAY* will be selling against them.

I'd like to add a word about newspapers generally. Their future is bright but they face challenges. Their biggest is selling against their competition. Many editors and publishers have recognized this and have already upgraded their paper's appearance, improved the editorial, and added new features and sections. Only by improving the product and encouraging marketing innovations will newspapers be able to maintain their competitive position as a medium for local and national advertising.

This is their biggest challenge – greater even than the technological and inflationary challenges of the recent past.

The need for newspapers continues to be strong. It is sad for the country, for the city, and tragic for those who lose jobs when a newspaper falls by the wayside. But declining newspaper readership should not be cited as the reason. For example, in Washington and Philadelphia, where papers closed recently, research indicates the surviving papers picked up approximately 85 percent of the defunct papers' circulation.[5]

This national newspaper began increasing its launching sites in major urban areas almost on a monthly basis, adding Greensboro, NC in February 1984 for the Carolinas, Tennessee, and nearby areas, and from Lawrence, Kansas, in April to serve Kansas, Missouri, Nebraska, and other related Midwest points. At that time there was a total of 24 *USA TODAY* print sites.[6]

Gannett Offset announced plans in January to build a printing facility at Chandler, Arizona outside Phoenix, to handle contract printing for the growing Southwest area. *USA TODAY* will be the plant's first major customer as it starts distribution in the fall of 1984 in Phoenix and surrounding Southwest areas.[7]

On the advertising front the newspaper averaged 8.3 pages a day in April 1983, about 20 percent ahead of projections, with 400 major companies participating.[8] In the fall of 1983 the 8.3 page average fell off and a series of top executive changes were made at the newspaper. These changes included moving Deputy Chairman John E. Heselden in as publisher and later adding Cathleen Black, formerly of *New York* magazine as president reporting to Heselden. Valerie Salembier, formerly of *Life*, *Newsweek*, and *Inside Sports*, was then named advertising director, with headquarters in New York City.[9]

Advertising started picking up in April 1984, with the April 3 issue carrying 12 pages of advertising. In the June 25, 1984 issue of *Advertising Age*, USA TODAY proudly announced that starting July 2, "the most colorful newspaper is getting more colorful." Starting July 2, 1984, four-color pages in all four sections would be available to advertisers, and every weekday four four-color spreads would also be available.[10]

One of the problems from the beginning in the sale of advertising in this national newspaper was the lack of an Audit Bureau of Circulations audit. This audit was finally officially released June 25, 1984. The figures issued showed that for the last quarter of 1983, average daily-paid circulation of the Gannett Company newspapers was 1,179,834. For the first quarter of 1984 ABC reported circulation from the publisher's statement at 1,332,974, a figure Gannett had been using in advertising sales presentations.[11]

These figures make the national newspaper the nation's third largest daily behind *The Wall Street Journal* and the *New York Daily News.*[12]

The Gannett Company has long been considered one of the best managed in the media industry, receiving many awards for excellence in management. As far as we may observe from the outside looking in, the Gannett executives follow basic management policies. These policies, although well known by most successful industrial leaders, are sometimes overlooked by executives. The new *Back to Basics, Management* outlines important precepts in decision making, a fundamental activity:

> Whatever managerial function is being performed, whether it is training, helping plan presentations, or building and maintaining morale, the manager-leader has to make judgments. His essential skill, therefore, has to be the ability to analyze, evaluate, and finally to make sound business decisions. It's a juggling act from beginning to end, and the manager leader who is able to keep more balls in the air, control them, and make them come down when and where he wants them to is the one who's going to win. Who said managing was easy? It's fun and it's challenging. But easy? No![13]

The leader of the Gannett Company, Allen H. Neuharth, is chairman of the board and has been with Gannett since 1960. He, too, has received many awards, and the company has financially rewarded him. In 1984 his total compensation from the company amounted to $1.25 million.[14]

Under Cathleen Black, publisher, and Valerie Salembier, senior vice-president, advertising *USA TODAY* has made unusual progress in attracting national advertisers.

The newspaper's total advertising pages through August 15 for the year 1985 were 1,947, up 69 percent from the comparable period a year ago. Advertising revenues were up 89 percent. The newspaper is now averaging 12.5 pages of advertising per issue according to Ms. Black.[15]

On August 27, 1984 the single copy price of *USA TODAY* increased from 25 cents to 35 cents, and its weekly delivered subscription price to $1.75 from $1.50. The newspaper's first quarter daily average paid circulation in 1984 has risen to 1,332,974, according to the publisher's unaudited statement.[16]

Gannett's corporate headquarters movedfrom Rochester, New York to Arlington, Virginia in mid-1985, when its Rochester lease expired.[17]

KEITH RUPERT MURDOCH

Rupert Murdoch, the Australian entrepreneur, now a U.S. citizen, has been making the newspaper world sit up and take notice for several years. This Oxford graduate and son of a distinguished editor owns the $1.4 billion News Corp Ltd. and has more than 80 publications and TV operations in Australia, Great Britain, and this country. His most recent takeover is the *Chicago Sun-Times* for $100 million.

While the price for the *Sun-Times* was high for a nonmonopoly newspaper, Murdoch received a lot for his money. At half the estimated revenues of $200 million, the profitable daily and Sunday newspapers seem like another one of Murdoch's timely buys, thanks to a quarrel between descendants of founder Marshall Field over the use of inherited assets. Along with the daily and Sunday newspapers, whose circulations exceed 600,000, Murdoch got some $30 million worth of real estate and two profitable news and feature services.[18]

Whatever his personal motivation, the 54-year-old Murdoch has always displayed a relentless devotion to getting things done. Starting with a small provincial newspaper inherited from his father, Murdoch combined skill and ruthlessness to build an international empire of 33 newspapers and magazines, including the *New York Post*, the *Times* of London and, most recently, the *Chicago Sun-Times*. His specialty has been to turn unlikely gambles into impressive profits.[19]

In addition to the stately *London Times*, he also publishes the authoritative daily *Australian*, the liberal *Village Voice*, and the gossipy but far from sensational *New York* magazine. To a degree that few people, least of all his fellow journalists, yet understand or even want to admit, Rupert Murdoch is an authentic heir of some great publishing figures of the past, such as William Randolph Hearst, Henry Luce, Joseph Pulitzer, and Britain's Lord Beaverbrook. While most media corporations today are run by relatively colorless, numbers-oriented businessmen, Rupert Murdoch, Australian born, British educated, but now domiciled in New York, almost alone among them combines a zest and a feel for the product with a shrewd sense of the bottom line.[20]

U.S. publishing	Acquired	Circulation
Daily newspapers		
Chicago Sun-Times	1983	639,134
Boston Herald	1982	317,612
New York Post	1976	962,078
San Antonio News and Express	1973	168,857
Weekly newspapers		
Houston Community Newspapers (7)	1979	253,988
The Village Voice (NY)	1977	155,834
Star (national)	founded 1974	3,824,792
Magazines		
New York (weekly)	1977	422,819

Australian publishing
    11 daily and Sunday newspapers
    16 other newspapers, most weeklies
    2 magazines
    2 book-publishing houses

British publishing
    4 daily and Sunday newspapers, including the *London Times*
    3 weekly newspapers
    2 book-publishing houses

Television
    2 stations in Australia
    Production company in New York

Other Communications
    Film- and record-production companies in Australia

Energy
    Offshore oil and gas exploration
    Natural-gas production and marketing

Travel and Transport
    50 percent interest in Ansett Transport Industries, a
        conglomerate that includes Australia's largest domestic
        passenger carrier, Ansett Airlines

Other
    Commercial printing in Australia and Britain
    Papermaking, paper warehousing, and shipping in Britain
    Interest in 6 newspapers in New Zealand

Source: "Murdoch Buys *Sun-Times*," *Newsweek*, November 14, 1983, p. 118.

What few people have noticed is that Murdoch's aptly named News Corp. already vies with Time Inc. and the Times Mirror Co. for world print leadership. News Corp.'s global revenues in the current fiscal year will approximate $2.1 billion, slightly behind Times Mirror's $2.5 billion and even close to Time Inc.'s $2.8 billion.[21]

Murdoch's Millions

Starting with a marginally profitable paper in Australia in 1952, Murdoch has built a $1.3 billion empire on three continents encompassing print and electronic media, filmmaking, energy production, and explorations and transport industries.

By most corporate publishing standards, Murdoch runs his operation like a one-man band. He keeps in close touch with most of his properties through detailed weekly financial reports, daily telexes from overseas, periodic visits, and endless phone calls, with blunt words of praise or scorn for a headline or an employee. He runs his newspapers on "a shoestring, fear and adrenaline," says one Australian staffer. There are tales of his dictating editorials, demanding that people be fired, but such direct control is hardly necessary. "He doesn't give explicit instructions," says one English journalist, "but he soon tells editors what he likes and dislikes – and they usually listen very carefully to what he says." Perhaps too carefully, some suggest. "Contemporary history is littered with the bodies of those who believed him on one issue or another," says former *Post* managing editor Robert Spitzler.[22]

NEWSPAPER COLOR

There is little doubt that the incursion of colorful *USA TODAY* into major markets has stimulated the recent upsurge in newspaper color. It appears that newspapers' next businesswide imperative is to establish uniformly excellent color reproduction. Color improvements in newspapers have been mandated by readers as well as advertisers.

The Newspaper Advertising Bureau has launched an ambitious program to do for color, on an industrywide basis, what was accomplished in standardizing ad sizes.

Working in conjunction with the American Newspaper Publishers Association's technical committee (chaired by Walter Mattson, president of the New York Times Co.), NAB's goal is to convince newspapers of the need to provide consistent color quality throughout their press runs and to offer that quality to advertisers on an industrywide basis.[23]

NAB has already conducted studies to "give some direction" to the color effort and presented some of its findings at the International Newspaper Advertising and Marketing Executives' convention in Miami, January 27-30, 1985.

One NAB study in December 1984 was based on 400 telephone interviews with ad agency executives and major advertisers to survey their attitudes toward color. Another study was based on six focus group sessions in three major markets to learn what color means to readers.[24]

National advertisers concede they often have excluded newspapers from their media schedules because of the medium's lack of uniform color quality. That was before the Gannett Four Color Newspaper Network.

An outgrowth of Gannett's nationwide *USA TODAY* – which spurred a cavalcade of color reproduction improvements throughout the nation's dailies – the newly formed network includes 95 newspapers that offer advertisers uniformly excellent process color.[25]

With one insertion order placed through the network, a national advertiser can place its ad in any combination of participating newspapers in the United States. The advertiser can schedule the ad in just one region, in one metropolitan group of newspapers, or throughout the entire network, which has a circulation of 9 million and 24 million readers.

The network officially was announced mid-March with a pullout promotion piece inserted in *Advertising Age*.

Any newspaper may apply for membership in the network, says William V. Shannon, senior vice-president, retail marketing, of Gannett Media Sales, New York City. The success of the network, in fact, will depend largely on the non-Gannett dailies that will flesh out its geographic map of distribution. Only 38 of the 95 network members are owned by Gannett.[26]

The newspapers "all have a dedication to quality . . . four-color advertising," Shannon says. "There is a great deal of excitement in the development of color standards and the coordinated effort to sell more newspaper color."

To earn a place in the network, a newspaper must pass a print quality test – a four-page broadsheet containing full-color ads for Merit cigarettes and Captain Morgan rum. So far, all qualifying newspapers have used offset printing.[27]

Computerized assistance for newspaper planners and buyers is also on the way. The numbers crunch in planning and buying newspaper space was eased earlier this year by the adoption of SAUs (standard advertising units, measured in inches and standard column formats). And further help is imminent from a system initiated last year by Doyle Dane Bernbach, with assistance from the sales reps, Kelly Story & Smith, and Sawyer, Fergusen, Walker. The data, which include ABC circulation figures and pricing, was made available by DDB for the top 50 markets in July. The system was expanded to include 100 markets by year's end, and by mid-1985 it will go up to 210. The data are presented in ADI (area of dominant influence) and DMA (designated market area) form and, with further work up, will be available in other geographical breakouts.

The DDB system has been offered to, and accepted by Telmar and Interactive Market Systems, both of which provide on-line data and planning software, and Management Science Associates, an on-line data service.

Agencies with newspaper-oriented clients have generally worked out computerized planning systems that meet their particular needs but have not shared them with the industry. The DDB system is open to broader applications than most of those specifically developed programs.

Computerization of newspaper data will save agencies and companies that do in-house media considerable time in the planning process. The systems can be further expanded to include agency billing and accounting procedures. DDB's Sy Goldis, senior vice-president and director of media services, finds "with this on-line data, planners can save up to 90 percent of the time it would take to do the calculations by hand." The preparation of a list, calculations of reach, and costs, can be reduced from 35 hours to three hours, estimates Goldis.[28]

RESEARCH

One share point of national advertising now represents almost $500 million in revenues. Although the final figures for advertising expenditures for 1984 have not yet been published, it has been projected that newspapers will have carried about $23.5 billion or 27 percent of the $87 billion total, more than any other medium.

That's the good news. The bad news is that almost 90 percent of it was in retail or classified. In 1983, newspapers ran only about $3 billion in national advertising, a 6 percent share. Clearly, national advertising represents a tremendous potential for newspapers.

One of the major steps our industry has taken to sell national advertising has been quality, syndicated research.

Although syndicated research had existed for the broadcast and magazine industry for many years, newspapers did not have an exclusive syndicated study prior to 1980.

Since then, and through the combined efforts of the International Newspaper Advertising and Marketing Executives and the Newspaper Research Council, several syndicated studies have been completed by Simmons and Scarborough. In 1983, Mediamark Research Inc. also included specific newspaper audience data in their reports. In June 1985 the 50+ ADI markets study by Simmons/Scarborough Syndicated Research Associates was released.[29]

FAMILY WEEKLY

Gannett Co.'s agreement to purchase *Family Weekly* from CBS Magazines has set off speculation as to what the new owner plans for the ailing Sunday magazine.

Industry insiders believe that, under the agreement reached February 21, 1984, Arlington, VA-based Gannett will pay between $35 million and $50 million for *Family Weekly*, which last year earned an estimated $6 million before taxes. These insiders say CBS had asked $60 million for the weekly.

What Gannett will get, just a month after it agreed to pay $200 million for the *Des Moines Register* and other newspaper properties of Des Moines Register & Tribune Co., is an admittedly ailing publication that CBS has been unable to turn around since its purchase in 1980, but it is a property that holds promise for a company like Gannett.

"It's kind of interesting," said John Morton, publishing analyst for Lynch, Jones & Ryan, Washington. "One wonders what's up Gannett's sleeve."

Mr. Morton did not have to wait too many weeks to learn what was "up Gannett's sleeve." The company decided to change the name of *Family Weekly* to *USA WEEKEND* and also to make changes in the magazine's format and editorial content. At the same time, Gannett signed up additional large city newspapers to take on the new supplement, such as the *Dallas Times Herald*, the *Denver Post*, and the *Chicago Tribune*.[30]

In 1984, according to Publishers Information Bureau, *Family Weekly*'s ad pages fell 11.2 percent, to 693 from 780, as ad revenues fell 10.4 percent, to $87.1 million from $97.2 million. So far in 1985, through the February 17 issue, ad pages are estimated to be down 0.2 percent.[31]

OLD-LINE NEWSPAPERS SELL TO BIG CHAINS

Dollars are winning out over sentiment as heirs of old-line publications sell to the big chains. Since 1945, the number of dailies owned by newspaper groups has risen from 368 to 1,169.

For as long as members of the Cowles family can remember, the *Des Moines Register* has been a cherished part of their legacy. Now, after four generations, they are parting with the newspaper and other media properties.

To some in the family, the sale to the giant Gannett chain, announced on January 31, is like the death of a close relative. "It is terribly sad," says Elizabeth Ballantine, great-granddaughter of Gardner Cowles, Sr., who brought the paper into the family in 1903. "We were educated to think of the newspaper as a family trust."[32]

But not all are mourning as a paper often ranked among the nation's best changes hands, with Gannett paying about $200 million for the *Register* and three smaller newspapers. "Everyone has had to weigh family ties against economic reality, and most put more weight on the latter," says Shawn Kalkstein, an advocate of the sale. His wife Karen is a fourth-generation Cowles.[33]

A Growing Trend

What is happening in Des Moines is by no means unique. In an age of big media conglomerates, papers and small chains controlled by families with deep roots in a community are increasingly rare. In 1983, the Congressional Research Service reports, only 531 of the nation's 1,700 dailies were independently owned, with most of these in family hands. Some other papers are part of media groups controlled by families.

Experts worry that the trend away from local ownership produces papers less responsive to the communities they serve. "Studies show that locally owned papers print more local news and are more involved with the community than chains," says Ben Bagdikian, professor of journalism at the University of California at Berkeley.

In the last few years, several major dailies have moved from family hands to ownership by corporations. In Chicago, the Field brothers sold the *Sun-Times* to publisher Rupert Murdoch, who is based in New York. Houston's Hobby family turned over the *Houston Post* to Canada's Toronto Sun Group, and the Miller family sold the *Allentown* (PA) *Call-Chronicle* to the Times Mirror Company of Los Angeles.

Many sales occur because of heavy estate taxes that can be paid only by putting papers on the block. Others take place when families, sometimes after painful soul-searching, decide that the financial gains override any attachment.

Almost anything has a price, says Quimby Melton, Jr., who in 1982 turned over the reins of the *Griffin* (GA) *Daily News* to the Thomson Newspaper Group. The paper had been in the family for 57 years before being sold to the Canadian firm for an undisclosed sum.

Family squabbles and lack of interest by heirs also lead to sales. In the case of the *Houston Post*, Jessica Hobby Catto, whose family sold the newspaper, says there just wasn't anyone in the next generation "who was the right one at the right time" to take over. So the family decided to concentrate on the broadcasting business.[34]

Another example of old-line newspapers selling out to large chains is the agreement by the Evening News Association of Detroit to sell the media group to the Gannett Company, Inc. for $717 million, ending 112 years of Scripps family ownership of the ENA media group. The announcement was made on August 29, 1985.

Besides the *Detroit News*, ENA publishes four daily newspapers, and owns five television stations.[35]

The *Detroit News* will be the largest daily circulation newspaper in the Gannett group. Its circulation is just over 650,000, daily, and over 800,000, Sundays.

NOTES

1. Walter Cronkite, address delivered to the Walter Cronkite School of Journalism and Telecommunication, Arizona State University, November 5, 1984.

2. Letter from Phillip Giolanella, president, and John Curley, editor, *USA TODAY*, August 27, 1982.

3. "Allen Neuharth: The Guru of Gannett," *Marketing and Media Decisions*, November 1982, pp. 64, 65.

4. *Advertising Age*, August 9, 1982.

5. Milton Rockmore, "How *USA TODAY* Rates as an Ad Medium," *Editor & Publisher*, March 31, 1984, pp. 16, 17, 29.

6. Gannett Company First Quarter Report, Chairman's Letter. 1984, p. 2.

7. Ibid.

8. *Editor & Publisher*, June 11, 1983, p. 100.

9. *Advertising Age*, April 9, 1984, p. 28.

10. *Advertising Age*, June 25, 1984, pp. 34, 35.

11. William Gloede, "*USA TODAY* Audit a Half: Agencies," *Advertising Age*, June 25, 1984, pp. 3, 118.

12. Ibid.

13. Mathew J. Culligan, C. Suzanne Deakins, Arthur W. Young, *Back to Basics Management*, pp. 27, 28. New York: Facts on File, 1983.

14. Gannett Notice of Annual Meeting of Shareholders to be held on May 21, 1985, p. 5.

15. Pamela G. Hollie, "Advertising," *The New York Times*, August 22, 1985, p. D-20.

16. *Editor & Publisher*, July 21, 1984, p. 39.

17. *Advertising Age*, July 23, 1984, p. 58.

18. Tom O'Hanlon, "What Does This Man Want?" *Forbes*, January 30, 1984, p. 80.

19. "Murdoch's Broadside," *Newsweek*, January 16, 1984, p. 59.

20. Ibid., p. 78.

21. Ibid., p. 79.

22. "What Makes Rupert Run?" *Newsweek*, March 12, 1984, pp. 71, 72.

23. Andrew Radolf, "Standardization of Color," *Editor & Publisher*, January 26, 1985, p. 8.

24. Ibid.

25. "Bringing National Advertising Color Back to ROP via the Gannett Four Color Newspaper Network," *INAME NEWS*, April 1985, p. 11.

26. Ibid.

27. Ibid., p. 12.

28. "A Shortcut for Newspaper Buying," *Marketing & Media Decisions*, January 1985, p. 52.

29. Steve Seraita, Research, "Using Research to Sell National Ads," *Editor & Publisher*, January 26, 1985, p. 16.

30. Gannett Company, Inc. Second Quarter, 1985 Report, p. 2.

31. William F. Gloede, "CBS Sells Off *Family Weekly*," *Advertising Age*, February 25, 1985, pp. 1, 82.

32. "Behind the Demise of Family Newspapers," *U.S. News and World Report*, February 11, 1985, p. 59.

33. Ibid.

34. Ibid.

35. "*Detroit News'* Parent Firm Agrees to Sale to Gannett for $717 Million," *The Arizona Republic*, August 30, 1985, p. H1.

8

THE LOS ANGELES TIMES

> For the *Times* ... the Olympics were an irresistible opportunity to show off its star writers, its new color presses and its enormous depth. ... It was, over all, a bravura demonstration of what a newspaper can accomplish when it is as packed with talent as it is with classified ads.[1]
>
> Jerry Adler, *Newsweek*
> August 31, 1984

EARLY HISTORY

Los Angeles, as we know it today, is said to have been founded in September 1781 by a group of 44 Mexicans who had traveled 1,000 miles by boat and land from Mexico and gathered on the banks of a narrow river.[2]

A hundred years later a strapping 6-foot-2, 200-pound Civil War veteran named Harrison Gray Otis strode into a small newspaper named the *Los Angeles Daily Times* in the summer of 1882, and began asking questions. The printers were looking for someone who could lift the burden of ownership of the *Times* off their backs.[3]

They soon struck an agreement with Otis and he became editor at $15 a week, and he would purchase one-fourth interest in the newspaper for $6,000, mostly secured by a bank loan.[4] It is difficult to comprehend that the great Los Angeles newspaper we know today had such humble beginnings.[5]

One Harry Chandler arrived in Los Angeles from New Hampshire in 1882 and among other activities began investing in *Times* delivery routes.

In 1887, at the age of 23, he was brought to work at the *Times* as a circulation clerk. In 1890 when the competing *Tribune* folded, Chandler sent a third party to buy the *Tribune*'s production equipment for about five cents on the dollar. This equipment was later purchased from Chandler by Otis, and Chandler was promoted to circulation manager and later business manager of the *Times*. He also married the boss's daughter, Marian Otis.[6]

Union troubles started at the *Times* when the typographical workers organized in 1886. When this union sought to deny the *Times* undisputed power over the hiring and firing of printers, Otis refused to go along.[7]

When the printers served notice they would leave, Otis told them to go. He hired 20 union busters known as the Printer's Protective Fraternity from Kansas City, and fired the unionists on the *Times*. Ultimately, Otis became the fountainhead of anti-union sentiment in booming Los Angeles.[8]

At 1:07 A.M. October 1, 1910, a series of dynamite blasts rocked the *Times* building and surrounding neighborhood. Both Otis and Harry Chandler were away from the building that night, although they were the obvious targets.[9]

Otis was in Mexico City, but Harry Chandler was less than a block away and rushed to the building. The building was engulfed in smoke and flames and walls collapsed all around. Many of the 100 employees on duty were saved, but 20 people perished and 21 others were injured.[10]

Chandler led a group of employees to an auxiliary printing plant and within five hours published a four-page issue with this headline: UNIONIST BOMBS WRECK *TIMES*: MANY SERIOUSLY INJURED. The building was rebuilt and the bombers brought to trial and convicted.[11]

When Harrison Gray Otis died in 1917 he left the *Times* to his daughter Marian Otis Chandler and his son-in-law Harry Chandler. Chandler was an astute businessman and he set about not only making the *Times* successful but achieved financial security for himself and his family through the acquisition of "solid" land.[12] He led the *Times* through a series of successful years and at the same time participated in numerous civic activities. He died in 1944.

In the meantime his oldest son Norman was beginning to learn the business, and finally, with two semesters left to finish at Stanford, left college and began to work full time at the newspaper. He also met and married Dorothy Buffum, who also was to play a most important role at the newspaper and in leading civic endeavors. One instance

A high speed Goss Metroliner press in action at the *Los Angeles Times*

of her newspaper influence occurred in 1940 when she and Norman Chandler were having lunch with Tom Cathcart, vice-president of *This Week Magazine* in Los Angeles, to break the news to him that they were planning to cancel *This Week* as their Sunday supplement and start their own magazine. Cathcart was prepared for this event, and presented the couple with a dummy of a home-and-garden-type magazine called *Home* and suggested they keep both magazines, since they each had a separate appeal. Mrs. Chandler said, "Tom's right," and that settled that.[13]

Norman Chandler worked his way up in the newspaper, becoming assistant general manager, general manager, and finally publisher. He directed the newspaper operation in a determined manner from 1944 to 1960, and at the same time displayed a most gentlemanly and courteous manner. He was the epitome of the successful executive and looked the part – a most handsome man. The author had the pleasure of visiting with him and working with him during the period from 1955 to 1960 while serving as an executive at *This Week Magazine*.

The *Times* climbed steadily in advertising volume and in circulation. However, in 1960, Norman Chandler decided it was time for Otis Chandler to move up to publisher of the *Los Angeles Times*. Norman Chandler walked to a podium at a civic gathering in Los Angeles on April 11, 1960, and made the announcement. Otis was then 32, his father was still a vigorous executive, and there was shock in the audience and consternation in the family, where at least some relatives felt Otis was too young, too liberal, and too untried.[14]

Otis Chandler was asked by columnist James Brady if he was surprised that day. Otis replied, "I knew only a few minutes before; my father told me we were going to this function, and just before we got there he told me. He was old school. You didn't become a publisher until you were 50. But the directors wanted him to take on company-wide responsibilities. And my mother wanted me to be publisher."

When he got up to the dais that day, Otis was overwhelmed.[15] Otis Chandler is rated highly as a newspaper executive by many experts in the business. David Halberstam says, "He is by any scale the ablest publisher in America in business terms."[16]

His family founded and controls a vast publishing and communications empire that stretches literally from coast to coast, with newspapers in Long Island, Connecticut, Dallas, Denver, and southern California; hard-cover and paperback book publishers in Manhattan; national magazines; western forests and paper mills; television and radio stations; and cable television systems. It is a company that's experimenting with electronic newspapers and more.

Otis has served as board chairman of all that, as well as editor-in-chief of the *Los Angeles Times*, a title he invented for himself three years ago when, at the age of 52, he stepped down as publisher and handed over the job to the first nonfamily member ever to hold it, an LBJ protégé from Texas named Tom Johnson.

The big, profitable, largely provincial and relatively undistinguished newspaper Otis Chandler took over in 1960 is today, by whatever reckoning, ranked in the top five, perhaps in the top three American dailies. It is more profitable than ever and it is very, very big. Daily circulation is 1.08 million; Sunday circulation is 1.3 million. The Times Mirror Company is completing a $215 million press expansion program, the largest in newspaper history and is adding editorial color.[17]

Otis Chandler broke a nearly 100-year-old tradition when he named W. Thomas Johnson, president and chief operating officer, publisher of the *Los Angeles Times* in 1980. Johnson is a University of Georgia and Harvard Business School graduate. Johnson had been general manager of the *Times'* CBS-TV station in Austin, Texas and later publisher of the *Dallas Times-Herald*, another Times Mirror property. He is now 44 years of age and according to Otis Chandler, "He has exceeded all of my expectations."[18]

In 1960, Norman Chandler relinquished direct participation in the direction of the *Times* to devote his full energy to the expansion and diversification of the *Times'* parent company, the Times Mirror Co. At the time of his death in 1973, Times Mirror had become one of the largest publicly owned publishing companies in the nation.

When Otis Chandler became publisher in 1960, the *Times* was stronger financially than any other newspaper in the United States. Chandler was determined to match this with editorial excellence. Under his leadership, the *Times* increased the number of its domestic and foreign bureaus from two to 31 and garnered seven more Pulitzer prizes.

A satellite printing plant was constructed in Orange County, the first such plant for any metropolitan newspaper in the country. The size of the newspaper itself was also expanded, making it the only U.S. paper to include seven separate sections daily.[19]

It is the most profitable media franchise in the country, generating some $680 million in revenue and $120 million in operating profits in 1983.[20]

In April 1984, Tom Johnson was named publisher of the year by *Adweek* in its "Special Report on Newspapers." As the *Adweek* special report went to press, the *Los Angeles Times* was awarded two Pulitzer prizes. The newspaper was also named to the number three spot on *Adweek*'s annual list of the ten best newspapers in the United States. The list was headed by *The New York Times*, and *The Washington Post* was second.[21]

PRESENT-DAY EXECUTIVES

Executives of the *Los Angeles Times*

Tom Johnson, publisher and chief executive officer
Donald F. Wright, president and chief operating officer
William F. Thomas, editor and executive vice-president
Vance L. Stickell, executive vice-president, marketing

James D. Boswell, vice-president, employee and public relations
William Niese, vice-president and general counsel
James B. Shaffer, vice-president and chief financial officer
Larry Strutton, vice-president, operations

Ken Chevis, director of information systems
John Mount, director of marketing research
Don Clark, director of classified advertising
James W. Duncan, director of employee relations
Joellen Kitchen, director of promotion and public relations
Donald J. Maldonado, director of display advertising
Charles J. Morrow, director of production

David L. Paulson, controller
Colin Lindsay, director of administrative services
Bert R. Tiffany, director of circulation
J. Willard Colston, chairman, Los Angeles Times Syndicate

Source: Los Angeles Times Public Relations Department, January 1984.

The *Los Angeles Times* has led all other newspapers in the nation in total advertising volume since 1955. The 1983 totals:

Top 10 newspapers in total advertising	Total Advertising – 1983
1. *Los Angeles Times*	154,456,435
2. *Chicago Tribune*	110,733,277
3. *Houston Chronicle*	108,614,519
4. *The Dallas Morning News*	95,744,202
5. *San Jose Mercury News*	93,151,643
6. *The Washington Post*	93,132,745
7. *The New York Times*	92,434,303
8. *Orange County Register*	89,325,102
9. *Atlanta Journal & Constitution*	82,844,655
10. *Rocky Mountain News* (Denver)	82,029,885

Source: Media Records, 1955-1983.

MISCELLANEOUS FACTS

In 1983, the *Times* published 4,158,611 individual classified ads, more than any other newspaper in the United States. Only a few other newspapers have published 4 million ads in one year, a feat that *Times* has accomplished 13 times. And, in four of those years, the *Times* published more than 5 million ads.

The editorial library of the *Times* houses more than 12.5 million clippings and 1.5 million photographs from past issues of the newspaper. It also stores almost 3 million negatives of *Times* photos.

In bringing readers graphic news coverage, *Times* photographers used more than 48,000 rolls of film in 1983.

The *Times'* fleet of delivery trucks is powered by clean-burning propane fuel, which results in cleaner emissions. Last year the fleet logged more than 7 million miles.

Publishing the *Times* required 394,549 tons of newsprint in 1983. With a typical roll of paper extending about 6.4 miles, this was enough newsprint to reach the moon almost 13 times. The *Times* uses newsprint made primarily from residual wood chips, as well as recycled newsprint.

More than 987,165 gallons of black ink were used in printing the newspaper in 1982.

Producing the *Times* involves the talents of more than 9,000 employees, as well as more than 3,000 home-delivery carriers.[22]

NAMED ONE OF TEN BEST AMERICAN DAILIES

Based on the highest standards of journalism, the *Times* has consistently ranked among the top ten newspapers in the United States.

In April 1984 *Time* magazine published a list of the ten best U.S. daily newspapers, using as criteria "imaginative staff coverage of regional, national and foreign issues; liveliness in writing, layout and graphics; national impact achieved through general enterprise, command of some particular field of coverage or a track record of training top-rank younger journalists."

Time, which made no attempt to rank the ten newspapers, listed them alphabetically as follows: *Boston Globe, Chicago Tribune, Des Moines Register, Los Angeles Times, Miami Herald, New York Times, Philadelphia Inquirer, St. Petersburg Times, Wall Street Journal, Washington Post.*

Also in April 1984, *Adweek* magazine named its ten best newspapers based on the judgment of a diverse panel of journalists and educators. The *Times* was named as one of the top three newspapers in the United States, just as it was in a similar survey by *Adweek* in 1981.

Everett Dennis, dean of the University of Oregon School of Journalism, said, "The *Los Angeles Times* is a great exemplar of journalism. It is comprehensive, thoughtful and very forward-thinking in terms of issues it deals with. It is a newspaper of power and importance."

Also in 1983, a survey of journalism educators across the United States conducted by *Advertising Age* magazine named the *Los Angeles Times*, along with *The New York Times* and *The Washington Post*, as one of the top three newspapers in the country.[23]

Top Ten U.S. Newspapers in Circulation, 1983

The circulation of the *Times*, the largest in the West, is the second largest among the nation's metropolitan newspapers on weekdays and the third largest on Sunday. The *Times* also leads all newspapers in the nation in home-delivered circulation.

Weekday circulation

1.	*New York Daily News*	1,487,944
2.	*Los Angeles Times*	1,072,500
3.	*New York Post*	972,077
4.	*The New York Times*	945,658
5.	*Chicago Tribune*	757,501
6.	*The Washington Postt*	734,944
7.	*Chicago Sun-Times*	653,781
8.	*The Detroit News*	649,672
9.	*Detroit Free Press*	632,090
10.	*The Philadelphia Inquirer*	540,615

Source: ABC Publisher's Statements, 3 months ending March 31, 1983.

Sunday circulation

1.	*New York Daily News*	2,046,644
2.	*The New York Times*	1,562,578
3.	*Los Angeles Times*	1,358,420
4.	*Chicago Tribune*	1,128,949
5.	*Chicago Tribune*	757,501
6.	*The Washington Post*	1,006,468
7.	*The Detroit News*	851,291
8.	*The Boston Globe*	779,134
9.	*Detroit Free Press*	777,846
10.	*San Francisco Chronicle*	698,995

Source: ABC Publisher's Statements, 3 months ending March 31, 1983.

NEW SUNDAY MAGAZINE

On October 6, 1985, the newspaper launched a revolutionary new Sunday magazine – revolutionary in that it was the first Sunday supplement in the country to be printed on the same slick paper and in the same "consumer" size as magazines such as *Time, Newsweek,* and

People. For the first time in its 104-year history, the *L. A. Times* used an outside printer – the same one, in fact, that prints the western regional editions of the newsweeklies.[24]

The launching of the *Los Angeles Times Magazine* caps the most exhaustive and expensive research project the *Times* has ever undertaken. "The Normandy landing was nothing compared to this," one *Times* executive said half-jokingly. Using its own 50-person staff and two outside research groups, the *Times* spent $1 million over the past two years to find out just what kind of magazine readers and advertisers might like. They tested stories, sample covers, ideas, and titles on dozens of "focus" groups. In one test, they sent a prototype of the new magazine to 15,000 homes of *Times* subscribers and telephoned them all the next Tuesday to find out what they thought. They even went door-to-door to question people who don't read the *Times* at all.[25]

"It's certainly the most important step this newspaper will take in the next ten to 15 years," says Glen Peters, *Times* advertising manager and director of the new magazine project. "We spared no expense."

And just what did they come up with after all this? It is not *The New York Times Magazine* West. The *L. A. Times* people say they weren't aiming for that. The final prototype of the new magazine is a 64-page, slick, soft-hitting amalgam of features celebrating the good things of southern California (the lead piece is a paean to L. A.'s polyglot culture) plus regular service columns on decorating, gardening, cooking, fashion, and pets carried over from *Home*, the *Times'* 45-year-old Sunday magazine supplement, which is being killed off to make room for the new one.[26]

Home, which went through a half-dozen permutations after a start as *Farm and Tractor* in 1917 and as *Home* in 1940, was once the most profitable independent magazine supplement in the country. Although it was only a "shelter" magazine, confined to stories about the home and its appurtenances, *Home* averaged 88 pages in the late 1960s and 1970s.[27]

But then it fell on hard times. Readers remained loyal but the ads dwindled, to the point where *Home* has been averaging only about 24 pages in recent months and was down to a skimpy editorial content of recipes, tips on sewing, and how to get rid of fleas.

"We were trapped," says *Times* publisher Tom Johnson. "*Home* was losing its appeal to advertisers. The focus was too narrow. So we had to either invent a new magazine or give up on magazines. I felt it was worth a gamble to try a new book."[28]

A professionally styled media kit was published by the *Los Angeles Times* Research Department in early 1984. Besides facts and figures and a demographic study by Simmons Market Research Bureau, Inc., it included a 70-page prototype of the proposed magazine.[29]

The enthusiasm for this new magazine is reflected in the following quote from the 1984 media kit:

The *Los Angeles Times* is offering advertisers an exciting new magazine for their marketing campaigns: *Los Angeles Times Magazine.* In addition to its broad editorial scope and full-color design, *Los Angeles Times Magazine* delivers the readership strength necessary for reaching the Los Angeles market. *Los Angeles Times Magazine*'s 2.8 million readers represent Los Angeles' most affluent, well-educated and better-employed residents.

Additionally, *Los Angeles Times Magazine* provides advertisers with one of the most cost-efficient media buys in Los Angeles. Compared to many regional, weekly, monthly and newspaper-distributed magazines, *Los Angeles Times Magazine* delivers the lowest cost per thousand households reached.

The marketing potential of *Los Angeles Times Magazine* is even more significant in light of the declining audience share of television networks in Los Angeles. Alternate viewing options provided by VHF and UHF stations, cable TV and videocassette recorders have been major factors in the erosion of network ratings, particularly during prime time.

Los Angeles Times Magazine is the optimal media selection, delivering the upscale readership, weekly immediacy and cost efficiency that are essential for successful marketing results in Los Angeles, according to the *Times'* promotion department.[30]

WHERE THE *LOS ANGELES TIMES* IS PRODUCED

The main editorial, business, and production departments of the *Times* are located in Times Mirror Square, a complex of buildings occupying an entire block in the heart of the Los Angeles Civic Center.

The *Times* is published with a sophisticated system employing computers, lasers, complex electronic devices, and the latest graphic arts technology. An advanced-copy processing and editing system has been developed to set type for the more than 78,000 pages that are produced annually. At the heart of the typesetting operation is a photocomposition system that can set type at the rate of 6,000 characters per second and 1,800 lines per minute. Display and classified ads are also produced electronically by computer-controlled photocomposition.

As the newspapers are printed, they stream off the presses and are moved by conveyors into the mailroom. There they are automatically counted, stacked, and tied into bundles by high-speed equipment developed by the *Times.*

Another set of conveyors moves the bundles to loading docks, where a fleet of propane-powered delivery trucks speeds the newspapers to independent home-delivery agents and to *Times* street-sales distribution centers throughout southern California.

The *Times* also utilizes plants in Orange County, where both the daily Orange County and San Diego County editions are published; and in the San Fernando Valley, which publishes the Valley edition. Built in 1968, the Orange County facility is located 37 miles from Times Mirror Square and houses a staff of more than 1,000 employees. The San Diego County edition is produced by a staff of 81 in San Diego County. The San Fernando Valley plant houses more than 600 *Times* employees.[31]

The Times Mirror Company, the parent company of the *Los Angeles Times*, reported a second-quarter 1984 net income of $58.9 million, or $.86 per share, an increase of 37 percent over the $43.0 million, or $.62 per share, recorded in the second quarter of 1983.

Revenues for the quarter were $705.9 million, up from $616.1 million in last year's second quarter.

In the first half of 1984, Times Mirror's net income totaled $102.2 million, or $1.49 per share, a 41 percent gain over the $72.5 million, or $1.05 per share earned in the first half of 1983.

Second-quarter operating profits of the newspaper publishing group increased 18 percent to $70.5 million from the $59.8 million earned in last year's second quarter. The *Los Angeles Times, Newsday*, the *Hartford Courant*, and Southern Connecticut Newspapers, Inc., all owned by the Times Mirror Company, recorded especially strong second-quarter results.[32]

LEADS ALL NEWSPAPERS IN TOTAL ADVERTISING

The *Los Angeles Times*, which has led all U.S. newspapers in total advertising volume since 1955, retained its top spot in 1984. The Times Mirror Co. flagship closed out the year with a record total of more than 198 million lines of display, classified and preprint advertising, a 17.3

percent increase over 1983. The *Times* carried more than 142 million lines of display advertising, an increase of more than 16.5 million lines, and a 13 percent jump over 1983 levels. The paper ran 55.8 million lines of classified advertising, a 12.3 million line increase over 1983, and 28 percent rise over the previous year's performance. In preprints, display advertising carried more than 54 million lines, a 28.5 percent boost over last year. Classified advertising preprint linage registered a more than 40 percent gain over 1983 with 1.3 million lines.[33]

ROBERT F. ERBURU BECOMES CHAIRMAN

Robert F. Erburu, president and chief executive of the Times Mirror Company, added the title of chairman January 1, 1986, the publishing company announced in March 1985. He succeeded Otis Chandler, great-grandson of the founder of the *Los Angeles Times*, the company's flag-ship newspaper. Mr. Chandler, 57, became chairman of the Times Mirror executive committee. He had been chairman of the company since 1981.

The changes, made as part of what the company described as "a long-standing management succession plan," were prompted by the retirement of Dr. Franklin D. Murphy, the current chairman of the executive committee.

Dr. Murphy, former company chairman and chief executive, turned 70 January 1986 making him ineligible for re-election to the Times Mirror board of directors.

Besides the *Times*, the company owns Long Island's *Newsday*, the *Denver Post*, and the *Dallas Times Herald*. It also publishes several magazines, including *Golf* and *Outdoor Life*, and owns several radio and television stations. The company had a net income of $232.7 million in 1984, a gain of 17 percent from 1983. Sales rose 12 percent last year, to $2.8 billion.

John Morton, an analyst with Lynch, Jones & Ryan, said he doubted that the shift in the chairman's office next year would result in much change in the company's direction.

"I'm convinced that Mr. Chandler will continue to have a strong influence on the company and its devotion to high journalistic standards in its newspapers and magazines," he said.

Mr. Erburu, who is 54, has an undergraduate degree in journalism from the University of Southern California and a law degree from Harvard. He was an attorney with the large Los Angeles-based firm of Gibson, Dunn & Crutcher before joining Times Mirror as general counsel and secretary in 1961.

Mr. Chandler was publisher of the *Los Angeles Times* for 20 years, starting in 1960, and is widely credited with broadening the newspaper's coverage and raising its reporting standards. He was chairman and editor in chief of the *Times* since 1981. He will yield those positions at the end of the year, the company said.[34]

NOTES

1. Jerry Adler, "Hometown Paper Makes Good," *Newsweek*, August 13, 1984, p. 30.

2. Marshall Berges, *The Life and Times of Los Angeles*, p. 3. New York: Atheneum, 1984.

3. Ibid., pp. 3, 6.

4. Ibid., p. 6.

5. Ibid.

6. Ibid., pp. 16, 17.

7. Ibid., p. 19.

8. Ibid.

9. Ibid., p. 21.

10. Ibid., p. 22.

11. Ibid.

12. Ibid., p. 34.

13. Personal interview with Tom Cathcart, vice-president, *This Week Magazine*, June 1, 1955, in New York City.

14. James Brady, "Otis Chandler: Always Seeking New Challenges," *Advertising Age*, May 16, 1983, p. M-38.

15. Ibid.

16. David Halberstam, *The Powers That Be*, p. 290. New York: Alfred A. Knopf, 1979.

17. James Brady, *Advertising Age*, pp. M-38, M-40.

18. Betsy Sharkey, "L.A. Times' Johnson: Publisher of the Year," *Adweek*, April 1984, p. 8.

19. *Los Angeles Times* files.

20. Ibid.

21. "L.A. Times' Johnson: Publisher of the Year," *Adweek*, April 23, 1984, p. 3.

22. *Los Angeles Times* files.

23. Ibid.

24. Karl Fleming, "The New *Los Angeles Times* Magazine, *Washington Journalism Review*, April 1985, p. 48.

25. Ibid.

26. Ibid.

27. Ibid., p. 49.

28. Ibid.

29. *Los Angeles Times* Research Department Media Kit, 1984.

30. Ibid.

31. "Facts About The Los Angeles Times," published by the *Los Angeles Times*, 1984.

32. "Times Mirror Profits Rise," *Editor & Publisher*, September 29, 1984, p. 59.

33. *Advertising Age*, February 18, 1985, p. 51.

34. *The New York Times*, March 7, 1985, p. 26.

9 ———————————————————

THE WASHINGTON POST

EARLY HISTORY

Eugene Meyer, who had purchased *The Washington Post* for $825,000 at a public auction June 1, 1933, made the following statement of principles to his staff on March 5, 1935:

> The first mission of a newspaper is to tell the truth as nearly as the truth may be ascertained. The newspaper shall tell ALL the truth so far as it can learn it, concerning the important affairs of America and the world. As a disseminator of news, the paper shall observe the decencies that are obligatory upon a private gentleman. What it prints shall be fit reading for the young as well as for the old. The newspaper's duty is to its readers and to the public at large, and not to the private interests of its owner. In the pursuit of truth, the newspaper shall be prepared to make sacrifice of its material fortunes, if such course be necessary for the public good. The newspaper shall not be the ally of any special interest, but shall be fair and free and wholesome in its outlook on public affairs and public men.

As an indication of the high stakes now involved in newspaper purchasing, Rupert Murdoch paid $100 million in November 1983 for the *Chicago Sun-Times*. Gannett Co. paid $200 million for the *Des Moines Register* and the *Jackson* (TN) *Sun* in February 1985.

The Washington Post was founded by an independent-minded Democrat, Stilson Hutchins, on December 6, 1877. It was printed at 914 Pennsylvania Avenue, N.W., and had a circulation of 10,000. The newspaper contained four pages and cost three cents a copy.[1]

Mary Hadar, assistant managing editor, in the newsroom of *The Washington Post*.

Luis Lazzo, pressroom superintendent, with one of *The Washington Post* modern presses in action.

The *Post* published its first Sunday edition in 1880. Joseph Pulitzer wrote for the *Post* when he was temporarily in Washington, and the then relatively unknown Theodore Roosevelt contributed a series of western stories to the *Post* which appeared without his byline.

In 1888 Hutchins purchased the *Daily Republican*, at that time the *Post*'s sole morning competition, and launched the *Evening Post* in the only attempt ever made by the *Post* to publish an afternoon edition.

The next year Hutchins sold the *Post* to Frank Hatton, a Republican cabinet member, and Beriah Wilkins, a former Democratic congressman. On June 15, at an essay awards ceremony on the mall, U.S. Marine Band leader John Philip Sousa introduced the "Washington Post March," which he wrote especially for the newspaper. It became an immediate popular hit and is still a marching band favorite today.[2]

Hatton and Wilkins moved the *Post* to a new building at 1335 E Street, N.W., next to the National Theatre in late 1893. John R. McLean, owner of the *Cincinnati Enquirer*, bought the newspaper in 1905. Under his leadership, *The Washington Post* increased its circulation and advertising and boosted its profits, but McLean's loyalty to the Democratic party colored his news judgments and caused the paper to lose much of its credibility and influence.

McLean died in 1916 and his son, Edward, became publisher. A crony of President Warren G. Harding, young McLean switched the paper's allegiance to the Republican party. Circulation dropped, advertising decreased, and finally the *Post* stumbled into receivership.[3]

On June 1, 1933, a public auction was held on the steps of the *Post*'s E Street building, and the newspaper was sold for $825,000 to Eugene Meyer, a California-born financier. Meyer was not an experienced newspaperman, but he had strong convictions about publishing a newspaper.[4]

Eugene Meyer's enlightened editorial policies and his business acumen began to turn *The Washington Post* around. In the first ten years after he took over, circulation trebled to 162,000, and advertising soared from 4 million to 12 million lines.

PHILIP GRAHAM

In 1946, President Harry S Truman appointed Eugene Meyer the first president of the International Bank for Reconstruction and Development. Meyer was succeeded at *The Washington Post* by Philip L. Graham, his son-in-law, who had been assistant publisher.[5]

Philip Graham was born July 18, 1915 in Terry, South Dakota. His parents later moved to the Everglades in Dade County, Florida, and Graham went to Miami High School and later enrolled and graduated from the University of Florida. After his undergraduate career at Florida he entered Harvard University Law School and graduated in 1939 tenth in a class of 400 and was president of the law review.[6]

He met Katharine Meyer, daughter of Eugene Meyer, in Arlington, Virginia and married her in 1940. In 1942 Graham joined the Army Air Corps as a private, served overseas in the South Pacific, and was discharged in 1945 as a major.[7]

When he returned to civilian life he accepted the position of publisher of *The Washington Post*, a job promised to him by his father-in-law before he left for overseas in 1943. The date was January 1, 1946, and he was only 30 years old.[8]

Graham took over a newspaper that had shown a total profit of $249,451 in the wartime years between 1942 and 1945. In circulation it was well behind its competition, *The Washington Star* and the *Times-Herald.*[9]

Advertising linage totaled barely a fourth of that in the city's four dailies. Just as Graham was attempting to learn the newspaper business his father-in-law, Eugene Meyer, now 70, was asked to be the first president of the World Bank by President Truman. Graham was now on his own and proved to Meyer in six months that he was capable of taking charge of the newspaper.[10]

On July 23, 1948, Meyer returned to the newspaper as board chairman. He also announced the transfer of voting stock to Philip and Katharine Graham. What he did not announce was that Philip Graham would now hold 3,500 shares and his wife 1,500 of the 5,000 voting shares. He explained, "You never want a man working for his wife."[11]

In 1946 the company had acquired the controlling interest in WTOP radio station in Washington, D.C. Then in 1950, to accommodate the growing newspaper, Graham built a new $6 million plant for *The Washington Post* at 1515 L Street, N.W., installing up-to-date presses and other new equipment. On June 20, he purchased Washington's CBS television station and changed the call letters to WTOP-TV.[12]

In March 1954 *The Washington Post* purchased its last morning rival in the city, the *Washington Times-Herald.* Circulation of *The Washington Post* and *Times-Herald* jumped almost overnight to 380,000.[13]

As the *Post* gained in advertising linage and circulation with Philip Graham at the helm, Eugene Meyer had withdrawn almost totally.

His health was deteriorating, and he died on July 17, 1959 at the age of 83.[14]

Philip Graham carried on in his usual quick-witted manner, exhibiting all the best qualities of leadership. Everyone on the newspaper knew he could step in and do their job with more flair and efficiency. Many employees were fond of saying, "I love that guy."[15]

As further evidence of Graham's foresight and desire to expand the company's communication enterprises, he began negotiations to purchase *Newsweek* magazine in New York. Benjamin Bradlee, who was later to become the famous executive editor of the *Post*, was then the Washington bureau chief of *Newsweek*. He made the original suggestion to Graham to purchase the newsweekly. The deal was consummated in New York on March 9, 1961. The magazine was purchased for $15 million. In 1983, *Newsweek*'s pre-tax profits alone amounted to an identical figure.[16]

It was evident to family and friends alike that Philip Graham was a manic-depressive and the symptoms were becoming more evident each month from 1960 on. Finally, after several voluntary stays at a private psychiatric center in Rockville, Maryland, and under a physician's care, he committed suicide on August 3, 1963, at the age of 48 while on a weekend visit to his farm.[17]

After the shock of Graham's death, felt by everyone close to him, including President Kennedy, Katharine Graham had an important decision to make.

"When my husband died I had three choices," she recounted. "I could sell it, I could find somebody else to run it, or I could go to work. Although 'the vultures were flying around' with offers to buy, it was simply inconceivable to me to dismantle all that my father and my husband had built with such labor and such love."[18]

On September 20, 1963, Katharine Graham assumed the company's presidency. During this difficult period she was fortunate to have Frederick "Fritz" Beebe by her side. He was an attorney, a member of the company's law firm who was soon to become chairman of the board of the Washington Post Company and of Newsweek, Inc.[19]

THE *POST* EXPANDS, 1966-1973

In 1966 the company bought a 45 percent interest in the *New York Herald Tribune*'s Paris edition. Later *The New York Times* joined

Whitney Communications and the *Post* as co-owners and renamed the property the *International Herald Tribune*.[20]

John W. Sweeterman was the publisher and executive vice-president of the newspaper at the time of Philip Graham's death. The newspaper was doing well under his regime, carrying about 49 percent of the total advertising linage of the three dailies. On March 1, 1969, Sweeterman, who had asked for early retirement, became vice-chairman of the board, and Katharine Graham took on the additional title of publisher. She chose Paul R. Ignatius, outgoing secretary of the navy, to be executive vice-president. He lasted less than two years.[21]

In 1969, the Washington Post Company purchased the ABC-affiliated television station in Miami, FL, and changed the call letters to WPLG-TV in honor of the late Philip L. Graham.

On June 15, the Washington Post Company offered the Sale of Class B common stock to the general public. Until then, the Post Company had been privately held. Its stock is now listed on the American Stock Exchange.

Frederick "Fritz" Beebe, the *Post*'s attorney and chairman of the board, sold the idea to Mrs. Graham that the Washington Post Company had to go public with a stock offering. The company was obligated to pay off in cash many millions of dollars in stock options and there was also the threat of devastating inheritance taxes should anything happen to the publisher; thus, a $33 million public class B stock offering was made. In light of recent tax difficulties encountered by the Newhouse family following S. I. Newhouse's demise, Beebe's advice was more than brilliant.

On June 18, *The Washington Post* began publishing excerpts of the "Pentagon Papers," containing secret information about the war in Vietnam. On June 30, the U.S. Supreme Court upheld the right of the *Post* and other newspapers to publish the "Pentagon Papers."

In ceremonies at Howard University in Washington, D.C., Katharine Graham donated radio station WTOP-FM to the university "to stimulate the intellectual and cultural life of the whole community and to train more people for the communications industry." On December 6, with the new call letters WHUR-FM, the station became the first under black management to broadcast in the Washington metropolitan area.

Early in 1972, a landmark story in American journalism started simply as a crime story off the police blotter. The breaking-in at the Democratic national headquarters at Watergate was to expand later into a classic example of dogged reporting by two young *Post* reporters, Carl

Bernstein and Robert Woodword.[22] *The Washington Post* may be better known by the American public for its coverage of this event than anything else in its history.

On October 16, 1972, an addition to *The Washington Post*'s building was dedicated, doubling the work area to more than half a million square feet.[23]

Early in 1973, Katharine Graham was elected chairman of the board and chief executive officer of the Washington Post Company while continuing as publisher of *The Washington Post* newspaper. In September the *Post* formed *The Washington Post* Writers Group to syndicate articles and publish books. The author served as a consultant to Benjamin Bradlee, Haynes Johnson, and others during the initial planning of this syndicate in 1972. Later, William B. Dickinson, Jr. was selected as editor and general manager of the new project. A dozen or so nationally recognized columnists, including George Will, Jane Bryant Quinn, and Ellen Goodman and the political cartoonist Tony Auth are now syndicated through the *Post* Writer's Group to more than 2,000 clients.[24]

LABOR RELATIONS, 1971-1975

In the fall of 1971 the Newspaper Guild negotiated a new contract with the *Post* that reinforced Mrs. Graham's belief that labor relations at her newspaper were deplorable. The Guild's negotiators simply outfoxed the company. The *Post* made a "final offer," but the union turned it down. The *Post* then amended it, but the union turned it down again, and the paper amended it again. Finally, the union accepted the proposal, which was a good deal better than the original "final" offer.

At about the same time, in late 1971, the printers began another slowdown. Their contract was to expire in 1972, and they began early to pressure the *Post*. Soon their protest escalated into the worst labor trouble the *Post* had ever experienced. This crisis will be described in some detail in this chapter.

The union, not surprisingly, saw it differently. It knew that the very future of the printer's profession had become an issue in its collective bargaining with the *Post*. The management might talk of efficiency, automation, new technology, and the like, but printers saw something else – the end of craftsmanship and of the printing process as it had been practiced for centuries.

What happened was a total disruption of the production of the *Post*. Type was deliberately misplaced; schedules were deliberately ignored.

Labor relations at the *Post* did not improve during the years 1973 through 1975. Finally, on the night of September 30, 1975, the pressmen struck the newspaper. The stereotypers had left for home at 2:15 A.M. on October 1, 1975, thinking there would be no strike. However, shortly after midnight the members of Local 6, who were working pressmen and stereotypers, gathered for a chapel (union) meeting. Around 4:00 A.M. that morning a small group of pressmen began to vandalize the pressroom and physically attacked James Hover, the night foreman.

What they did, according to the *Post*, was damage that eventually cost $270,000 to repair: they sliced the cushions on the press cylinders, ripped out electrical wiring, removed key pieces of the folders on almost every press, jammed the cylinders, cut air hoses, and sabotaged other parts.

The most serious damage was caused by a fire, apparently started with gasoline on one unit of a new press. Whoever started the fire first partially disabled the automatic fire extinguishers on that press and an adjacent one. The fire melted the lead plates that were left on the cylinders, and spread to the rolls of newsprint in the reel room below. There the automatic extinguishers worked, and the fire did not spread. Had it spread just a few yards it could have reached a storage area which contained 121 huge rolls of newsprint.[25]

Following this violence, and the immediate institution of a picket line, negotiations with the union came to a standstill, and moved very slowly after that. The *Post* began to train employees in the old type production methods and to make plans to have the newspaper printed elsewhere and brought to the top of the building via helicopter.[26]

Employees worked day and night on "Project X" as it was called, including Mrs. Graham herself. Mark Meagher replaced John Prescott in 1974 as the man in charge of the *Post*'s day-to-day business operations.[27]

One of the advantages that the *Post* enjoyed at this point was the support of a majority of the Guild. These employees were repelled by the violence in the pressroom. Another advantage was that the *Post* seized the public relations initiative. Its third advantage was its ability to publish a newspaper without union labor. Before October 1, the *Post* employed 1,220 craft workers to put out a daily newspaper; from October 1 through February 16, it performed the task with a makeshift work force of 210 to 375. The newspaper is delivered by independent, non-union circulation dealers-entrepreneurs who contract with the newspaper to distribute it. The *Post* defied its craft unions and prospered without them, missing only one day of publication despite the damage to its presses.[28]

On the night of February 16, 1975, mailers and printers began to return to work. The February 18 edition of the *Post* was printed the traditional way, in hot metal. Angry members of Local 6 continued to picket outside the *Post*, but to no avail. Except for them and a handful of supporters from other unions who refused to cross their picket line, the strike had ended, after 139 days.[29]

FREDERICK BEEBE

In doing the research for this book and working under Frederick S. Beebe for years at *Newsweek*, the author has come to the conclusion that the press and book authors have not given this gentleman, who served as chairman of the board until his death on May 1, 1973 at the age of 59, nearly enough praise and credit for his outstanding contributions to this company in so many areas. For instance, he was responsible for the closing of the Washington Post Company's deal for the purchase of WSFB-TV in Hartford, CT, just prior to his death. While visiting with Mrs. Graham after her speech at a *Newsweek* sales meeting, the author asked her about the purchase and she gave Frederick Beebe full credit stating, "Fritz is one great negotiator." The *Post* named the call letters after him. In 1976, after working at the *Post* in various editorial, pro- duction, and executive capacities, Donald E. Graham, Katharine Graham's son, was appointed executive vice-president and general manager of the paper. Before joining the *Post*, Donald, who was a graduate of Harvard, spent two years on the Washington Police Force, on patrol, which gave him an unusual opportunity to learn and observe the various elements of the city.

Donald Graham became publisher of the *Post* in 1979, succeeding his mother, who retained her corporate positions of chairman of the board and chief executive officer of the Washington Post Company.

FURTHER EXPANSION

The Washington Post celebrated the 100th anniversary of its founding in 1977. The newspaper's Sunday supplement, *Potomac Magazine*, became the *Washington Post Magazine,* and a new Friday tabloid section, *Weekend,* was begun. In November, the Washington Post Company announced the sale of its one remaining radio station, WTOP-AM.

The Washington Post Company purchased the *Everett* (WA) *Herald,* a daily newspaper north of Seattle in 1978. Later, the Post Company announced an agreement to participate in a limited partnership with Dow Jones & Company and the Bato Company, Inc., to construct and operate a newsprint mill near Richmond, VA. In July the Washington Post Co. exchanged television station WTOP-TV in Washington, D.C., for WDIV-TV in Detroit.

On April 14, 1980, *The Washington Post* began publishing each Monday a financial tabloid section called *Washington Business.* The new section added approximately 15 columns of news and tables to the Monday business and finance pages that it replaced.

PRINTING AND CIRCULATION

To accommodate the *Post*'s growing circulation and conversion to cold type, the $60 million Springfield (VA) satellite printing plant was formally opened on November 12, 1980. The 315,000 square foot building houses three eight-unit offset presses, a revolutionary platemaking system, and a computer-controlled distribution system to route newspapers into delivery trucks. The presses can produce 128-page newspapers at approximately 75,000 copies per hour. Two of them are Goss presses and the third was manufactured by the Japanese firm of Tokyo Kikai Seisakusho (TKS). Completed pages are passed through EOCOM laserite machines at the downtown plant and are received in Springfield in negative form via microwave signals. The negative is then exposed to make an offset printing plate ready for the presses.

The *Post* is also printed at a second satellite facility located in southeast Washington.[30]

In March 1981 the *Post* changed its platemaking process for its nine downtown web presses from the stereotype method, which used lead heated to approximately 600°F to form a 50-pound printing plate, to a NAPP direct platemaking process. This process produces a very light plastic plate ready for the presses and provides reproduction similar to offset quality printing.[31]

The Washington Post is printed on nine web presses located on the ground floor of the *Post* building. The two newest Goss Mark II presses, installed in 1972, cost about $2.5 million each, took nine months to install, and are capable of printing 128 pages at once. These newer presses can print, cut, and fold 65,000 newspapers per hour. The seven other presses run at slightly slower speeds and print up to 112 pages at a time.

The daily circulation of the *Post* is 747,676 and of the Sunday edition is 1,005,468. Approximately 6,000 newspaper carriers working with 350 agents/distributors are responsible for home delivery.[32]

THE NEW LOOK

The Washington Post completely redesigned its news sections in the fall of 1984, for the first time since the late Eugene Meyer bought the newspaper in 1933. "We felt it was time for a new look, emphasizing readability, clarity, organization and order," said Executive Editor Benjamin C. Bradlee.

One of the most obvious improvements is an index occupying one-quarter of page 2, where it will appear daily. Previously, the *Post* had an index that was so brief it could be run in a front-page ear.

The *Post* also created a new format for columns of opinion and commentary in the news sections. The aim is to emphasize the distinction between news stories and the columns. Now the columns are boxed with bold Franklin Gothic headlines and are set in distinctive body type.[33]

The *Post* also announced:

New and enlarged mastheads for most inside sections. Metro, Sports, and Business mastheads are set in Bauer Bodoni type. Bodoni italics are used in the mastheads for the daily Style section and the Travel and Show sections on Sunday and the Food sections on Wednesday and Sunday.

A new headline style making more frequent use of smaller headlines under the main heads.

Bylines are standardized in full-size sections with rules above and below the writer's name.

Key boxes on the front pages of some sections referring to stories on the inside.

In announcing the changes, the *Post* also noted that in July it switched its body type to Century Oldstyle to aid production as the paper shifted to standard advertising units.

The changes were made in consultation with Walter Bernard and Milton Glaser of WBMG, Inc., New York, who separately or together had redesigned *Time, Esquire, Fortune, Atlantic Monthly, New York,* and *Adweek* magazines. Bernard and Glaser worked for a year on the *Post* project.[34]

The *Post* began publishing a new spin-off entitled *The Washington Post National Weekly* on November 7, 1983. Although it appears to be an editorial and circulation success with a weekly compendium of national stories and cartoons, some by its own premier reporters, it has not been an advertising success. It averages about two pages a week in a 40-page publication but has a circulation of 40,000.

Richard I. Simmons, age 49, has been president and chief operating officer of the company since September 1, 1981. Prior to joining the company, Mr. Simmons had for more than five years been a senior executive of the Dun and Bradstreet Corporation. His salary plus bonus in 1983 totaled $473,469.[35]

The Washington Post's operating income in 1983 increased 39 percent, to $79 million, from $57 million in 1982. Revenue for the division rose 10 percent, to $456 million, from $414 million the prior year.

The *Post*'s average Sunday circulation reached 997,000 for the six months ending September 30, 1983. This is a 2.5 percent increase over the September 1982 figure, and 26.7 percent above Sunday circulation five years ago. Average daily circulation of 719,000, though 1 percent less than in 1982, is 28.5 percent above daily circulation in 1978.

Advertisers benefited from the *Post*'s growing audience, which is the best-educated and most affluent among the country's top ten markets. Total advertising linage rose 2.8 percent, to 104 million lines, with particular strength in pre-prints and classified, and advertising revenue increased 13 percent to a new record high.[36]

In a joint statement dated February 24, 1984, in the Post Company's 1983 annual report, Katharine Graham and Richard Simmons wrote as follows:

The strength of our businesses, their capacity for growth and the encouraging potential of new fields make us confident that the Washington Post Company will have good results again in 1984. We believe the company is well positioned to achieve sustained earnings growth in the years to come.

However, there is an issue of concern that affects not only our future, but the future of all citizens. We refer to growing threats to freedom of the press in this country.

These threats are reflected in considerable public distrust and dislike of the media. They are felt in an alarming rise in the number of libel suits that go to trial, with concomitant heavy legal fees and onerous sums awarded to plaintiffs by trial juries. They are seen in the refusal to allow press coverage of the invasion of Grenada, as well as in recent attempts to limit the Freedom of Information Act, to classify more government documents and to censor the publications of many government officials.

All of these could undermine the ability of the media to do their job – to keep the American public informed about events that mold the future. The potential consequences are severe. If the news media are restricted, so, too, is the ability of people to understand and influence the course of their lives. If freedom of the press is sacrificed, so, too, is the freedom to govern ourselves that Americans have enjoyed for more than 200 years.

We recognize a heightened obligation to be fair, accurate and professional in reporting the news and in correcting our mistakes. At the same time, we are committed to defending First Amendment rights – the rights of people to have the most penetrating and illuminating information we can provide.[37]

NOTES

1. *The Washington Post* files, 1984.
2. Ibid.
3. Ibid.
4. Ibid.
5. Ibid.
6. Chalmers M. Roberts, *The Washington Post, The First 100 Years*, p. 256. Boston: Houghton Mifflin Company, 1977.
7. Ibid., p. 257.
8. Ibid.
9. Ibid., p. 258.
10. Ibid.
11. Ibid.
12. *The Washington Post* files, 1984.
13. Ibid.
14. Ibid.
15. Roberts, *The First 100 Years*, p. 321.
16. W. Parkman Rankin, and Eugene Sauvé Waggaman, *Business Management of General Consumer Magazines*, 2d ed., p. 112. New York: Praeger Special Studies, 1984.

17. Roberts, *The First 100 Years*, p. 363.

18. Ibid., p. 369.

19. Washington Post Company files, 1963.

20. Ibid., 1966.

21. Roberts, *The First 100 Years*, pp. 396-97.

22. David Halberstam, *The Powers That Be*, pp. 606, 607. New York: Alfred A. Knopf, 1979.

23. *The Washington Post* files, 1973.

24. Ibid.

25. Robert G. Kaiser, "The Strike at *The Washington Post*," *The Washington Post Outlook*, February 29, 1976, p. 7.

26. Ibid., p. 11.

27. Ibid., p. 12.

28. Ibid., p. 15.

29. Ibid., p. 19.

30. Ibid.

31. Ibid.

32. Publisher's Statement submitted to Audit Bureau of Circulations, for six months ending March 31, 1983.

33. "Washington Post Redesigns for First Time Since 1933," *Editor & Publisher*, November 3, 1984, p. 17.

34. Ibid.

35. Notice of Annual Meeting and Proxy Statement, 1984, Washington Post Company, pp. 4, 11.

36. Washington Post Company Annual Report, 1983, p. 2.

37. Ibid., p. 6.

10

The New York Times

*To give the news impartially, without fear or favor.
Regardless of any party, sect or interest involved.*[1]

Adolph S. Ochs

EARLY HISTORY

The first *New York Times*, published by a David Longworth and printed by Nicholas Van Riper, saw the light of day in 1813. It died almost a-borning. The only known copy is in the British Museum.[2]

There were other unsuccessful attempts at publishing a "Times" newspaper, including a semi-weekly and a Sunday edition. In all, seven attempts failed.[3]

Henry Jarvis Raymond, 31 years old, started the first successful venture of *The New York Daily Times*, in an old building at 113 Nassau Street on September 18, 1851. The price per copy was one cent, and it was neatly printed with a certain aura of dignity. It is interesting to note that the financial backing or encouragement for this new publishing venture came, not from Wall Street or publishing interests in New York City, but rather from two bankers in Albany, George Jones and Edward B. Wesley.[4]

During the early months Jones and Wesley alternately served as the business head of the newspaper. In these early days Raymond instituted a circulation sampling program door to door not unlike those carried on by present-day newspapers. Advertising came in with a rush in the beginning, and after the first year of operation it was evident that the

Times was on its way to a profitable future. To celebrate the daily price went up to two cents.[5]

Raymond continued his interest in politics while at the same time publishing a vital, growing newspaper. He became a congressman, but at the close of the Thirty-ninth Congress decided to give up politics. On June 19, 1869, Raymond died of an apoplectic stroke at the age of 50. George Jones took over the editorial as well as the financial end of the newspaper after Raymond's death. The newspaper's stock had gone from $1,000 a share to $11,000. Offers as high as $1 million were offered for the newspaper but Jones turned them down.[6]

George Jones set himself up as the first great businessman-publisher. This type, unlike the fire-eating newspaper owners of the past such as Webb, Bennett, Greeley, and Raymond, were destined to take over almost everywhere.[7]

Jones was born in a farmhouse in Poultney, Vermont. He went to New York in 1841 at the age of 30 and started in the offices of Greeley's *Tribune*. Of the 100 existing shares of *New York Times* stock, Jones had 30 shares and the Raymond family held 34. Raymond's son, Henry Warren, had graduated from Yale and had earned an A.M. degree and studied law at Columbia, but he never showed any of his father's flair for business or editing.

At one point in early 1871, Henry Raymond's widow, who held the 34 shares of stock, threatened to sell out to the Boss Tweed machine in New York. When George Jones received word of the pending deal, he contacted Col. E. D. Morgan, one of the original investors in the *Times*, and Morgan met with Mrs. Raymond and bought her shares for $357,000.[8]

George Jones died August 12, 1891. He had hoped that his heirs would carry on, but they were not so inclined. They sought to dispose of the newspaper as soon as possible. It was staggering and going downhill.[9]

The newspaper's unpopular political leanings, the cost of a new building, and the panic and depression of 1893 seemed to be death blows. Jones' sons sold out to an Edward Cary and Charles Ransom Miller, editor-in-chief, for $1 million.[10]

ADOLPH S. OCHS

Adolph S. Ochs was only 14 years old when he started in the newspaper business as a "printer's devil" on the *Knoxville* (TN)

Chronicle. Although his family was well-off when he was a boy, his father, who was in the textile business, lost everything when the bottom fell out of the textile market in 1867 during a year of panic in the South.[11] Young Ochs worked hard, and was a quick study. After four years at this job he began to look for greener pastures.

Late in 1877 Franc M. Paul, *The Knoxville Tribune*'s business manager, and Col. John Encil MacGowan, editor of the *Tribune*, banded together with young Ochs as their business solicitor and launched *The Chattanooga Dispatch.*[12]

In the spring of 1878, it was evident that *The Chattanooga Times* was in trouble. It was owned by S. A. Cunningham, who was also editor. Ochs saw an opportunity and asked Col. MacGowan for moral support. He tried to buy the newspaper, but Cunningham insisted on $800 cash. Eventually Ochs got a half-interest for $250 cash, with the right to buy the second half in two years. Ochs was just 20 years old at the time.[13]

By 1882, the Chattanooga newspaper prospered so much that Ochs ended up paying $5,500 for the second half of the *Times.* It was about this time that Ochs began spending a great deal of time in New York City, arranging financial deals and even making speeches at various affairs.

In the spring of 1896, Ochs was summoned to New York again by a personal friend, Leopold Wallach, a prominent member of the New York bar. At first the *Mercury*, a newspaper in New York, was being considered as a purchase, but the idea was abandoned. The *Mercury* soon thereafter ceased publication.[14]

A Mr. Harry Alloway, a member of *The New York Times* Wall Street staff who had known Mr. Ochs for six years, sent him a telegram on March 12, 1896, Mr. Ochs' thirty-eighth birthday, stating that if he was interested, there seemed to be a likely opportunity to buy *The New York Times* with no very large outlay of money.[15]

After many meetings and discussions with principals involved, a reorganization committee was formed, with a Mr. Spencer Trask acting as chairman. A new organization, the New York Times Company, was formed.[16]

As a persuasive, 15 shares of stock were offered to each purchaser of a $1,000 bond. Mr. Ochs bought $75,000 of these bonds, receiving with them 1,125 shares of stock. Of the remaining capital stock of the company, 3,876 shares were put into escrow to be delivered to Mr. Ochs whenever the newspaper had earned and paid expenses for a period of three consecutive years. In less than four years he had 5,001 of the 10,000 shares and $75,000 in bonds.[17]

The company then bought the *Times* at public sale on August 13, 1896, with Adolph S. Ochs as publisher in unrestricted control.[18] Ochs directed the activities of this New York City newspaper, much as he had his newspaper in Chattanooga.[19] Advertising was solicited and the volume increased. The Spanish-American War created some economic problems, but after a newspaper price increase from one cent to two cents was announced October 10, 1898, the prosperity of the *Times* was assured. Of the fact of success, there was never (from the end of 1898) any doubt.[20]

The growth of the newspaper under Mr. Ochs soon forced a move to larger quarters. In 1905, after the City Board of Aldermen changed the name of Longacre Square to Times Square in its honor, the *Times* moved into the Times Tower at Forty-second Street. Built by the *Times* for itself, it was the first skyscraper in the neighborhood. The newspaper quickly outgrew its new home and, in 1913, the *Times* opened an annex at 229 W. Forty-third Street, its present headquarters.[21]

Mr. Ochs, as he was called by all staff members, and even fellow top executives, continued to publish a most successful newspaper. In 1913 as fighting in Europe broke out in World War I, the *Times'* circulation was 242,000 daily and 158,000 Sunday. In 1918 the last year of the war, the daily had increased to 352,000 and the Sunday edition was over 486,000. The *Times* was even more dominant as a newspaper of an influential and expanding class.[22]

When Adolph S. Ochs died in 1935, the *Times* was one of the world's most influential newspapers. Under the leadership of Mr. Ochs' son-in-law, Arthur Hays Sulzberger, Mr. Sulzberger's son-in-law, Orvil E. Dryfoos, and later Mr. Sulzberger's son, Arthur Ochs Sulzberger (the present publisher and chairman) the *Times* has enhanced its reputation.

The 1930s were the years in which the *Times* solidified its position in New York and environs. In 1927, just prior to the Great Depression, there were 12 newspapers in New York City and three in Brooklyn. During the depression newspapers were dying all around the *Times*. By the mid-1930s it was obvious that the *Times* was locked in a struggle with another strong morning newspaper, the *Herald Tribune*, which was very much like the *Times* in tone.[23]

Mr. Ochs had taken the *Times* well into the new century, but it was during the reign of his son-in-law, Arthur Hays Sulzberger, that the *Tribune* was finally beaten. Sulzberger became publisher in May 1935, one month after Ochs' death. Sulzberger's wife, Iphigene, had inherited many of her father's characteristics, and for years was a most important influence on the policy-making decisions. Of the four publishers of the modern *New York Times* she was the daughter of one, the wife of the second, mother-in-law of the third and mother of the fourth.[24]

At the start of World War II, the *Times* and the *Tribune* were about even in profits and close in circulation. The *Times* daily was at 481,000 circulation, the *Tribune* at 347,000. The author became a member of the *Tribune*'s advertising staff in June, 1941. It was obvious that the *Tribune* under the direction of Helen Rogers Reid envied the retail advertising linage of the *Times*. She had hired William Robinson as advertising director at $30,000 a year. He later became president of the Coca-Cola Company in Atlanta. She also hired, away from the *Times*, Dan Provost as national advertising manager. When paper rationing went into effect in 1942, the *Tribune* opened its pages to more department store advertising and the *Times* expanded its news hole instead.

Although it appeared that the *Tribune* was moving ahead in profits and linage, it was a short-lived victory. By increasing its editorial coverage of World War II, the *Times* solidified its hold on the newspaper readers and it moved ahead, never again to be threatened by the *Tribune*. The *Times* led in Sunday circulation in 1950 by 675,000 to 1,173,000, and in 1960 by 521,000 to 1,371,000.

OPERATING PROBLEMS

During the ten years from 1955 to 1965, net income from operations at the *Times* averaged only 1 percent of total revenue. This unsatisfactory after-tax profit caused concern to management since they recognized that there must be a continuing program for improving operating efficiency to offset persisting increases in labor and material costs.[25]

The executives of *The New York Times* decided to call in the well-known management consultant firm Booz, Allen, & Hamilton for a six-week period to conduct a study of operations. The object of the study was to determine what cost reductions were possible, how much could reasonably be invested in a solution, and what direction or course of action should be taken.[26]

In order to complete the task successfully within the six-week span, it was necessary to establish a task force cost-reduction study team. The team was comprised of seven department heads from the *Times* and one Booz, Allen, & Hamilton consultant. The latter was to provide leadership, technical assistance, and experience to the team leaders.[27]

The majority of the team had never been called on previously to assist in a cost-reduction survey. Therefore, it was essential to develop a logical and systematic approach. This was accomplished by developing a preplanned work sheet and set of questions to aid and guide the leaders in their interviews with other department heads. This predeveloped approach was designed to prevent each leader from going his separate way in analyzing the department and thereby achieving a hit-or-miss analysis. It also channeled his approach to ensure that more than a cursory look would be given to each functional group of employees in a department.[28]

In 19 elapsed working days, 28 major departments, made up of over 100 individual cost centers, were examined. During that time, 128 separate cost-reduction opportunities were identified. The estimated potential yearly savings ranged from $7.1 million to $8.3 million. To achieve these cost improvements, a one-time cost of approximately $3.8 million would be required. A detailed summary of potential savings is shown for three classifications below.[29]

Originally, it had been believed that automation would be responsible for a major share of the cost-reduction opportunity. On the contrary, it was found that automation accounted for only 20 percent of the total potential annual savings.

During the course of the survey, many projects were identified that cross one or more departmental boundaries. The time limitation prevented a complete examination of them and, therefore, no dollar appraisal was assigned to them. Typical examples were satellite plant printing, analysis of display ad processing, analysis of restaurant operation, and information storage and retrieval systems.[30]

As a result of the recommendations developed from the survey, a staff services department was created. Three full-time employees from the *Times* were assigned to this department. In addition, five Booz, Allen, & Hamilton consultants worked on projects identified in the survey phase.[31]

The projects were divided into the following three classifications:

1. *Projects that could be implemented by the departments concerned without staff assistance.* In the first quarter of 1966 there was successful implementation on projects that amounted to $250,000 on an annual basis.
2. *Projects that required work by industrial engineering staff.* The projects in this category were being worked on almost exclusively by

Booz, Allen consultants. The fact-gathering segment of the majority of projects was complete. A process of designing and evaluating alternative methods, equipment, and systems was undertaken.

3. *Projects that required staff help that was to be provided by* Times *people.* Two major projects were analyzed. One was concerned with automating the newsprint storage system. The other related to advancing the printing schedule to reduce the peak and valley staffing situation.

Each of the above three classifications had potential savings in excess of $1 million annually for the feasible projects.[32] The various projects proceeded on schedule and the cost-reduction estimates made during the general survey by the consulting firm were realized.

Another management problem appeared almost ten years later:

By 1975 operating profit at *The New York Times* had fallen to $4,834,000 on revenues of $260,106,000. In order to maintain the traditional level of quality at the *Times*, executives of the *Times* believed that major changes would be required in several areas. They believed that the two most important areas were (1) introduce new technology in the form of automated composition and new presses, and (2) make the newspaper more attractive to regular subscribers. In order to monitor and control those changes, however, executives of the *Times* felt that improved planning and budgeting systems would be essential. The *Times* had prepared budgets since 1965, and in 1972 the newspaper developed its first long-range plan. In 1975, however, both the planning and the budgeting processes were considered to be very weak. According to Dr. Leonard Foreman, director of planning and chief economist, those processes were improved gradually over a period of several years.[33]

The change was in two steps, according to Dr. Foreman.

The first was primarily technical, while the second dealt more with people. Initially, we needed to improve our economic forecasting and our computerized budgeting system. The first technological change involved economic forecasting. Initially we used an outside consulting firm for our forecasting. Now we do quite a bit in-house, but we still use the consultant. Forecasts for inflation are used to budget expenses, while both area and general economic forecasts are used for subscription and advertising revenue budgets.[34]

The second technical change involved our budgets. Because of the size of *The New York Times*, we needed to have our budgets computerized. We now have both budgeted and actual expense on the computer by eight digit account number. The first four digits refer to department number. We have over 800 departments. The second four digits refer to expense category.[35]

OTHER INVESTMENTS

In 1980 the *Times* began production of a satellite national edition which is now printed in Chicago, Florida, Texas, and California.

In addition to *The New York Times*, the company publishes a number of regional daily and weekly newspapers, leading magazines, and books; operates a news service, television and radio stations, and a cable television system; and holds substantial equity positions in four newsprint companies. In 1984 the New York Times Company ranked 281 on the *Fortune 500* list.[36]

Net income of the New York Times Company in 1983 reached a new high: $78.7 million, or $2.02 per share, a 45 percent increase over $54.3 million in 1982, or $1.44 per share.

And for the first time, it became a billion-dollar company. Revenues of $1.1 billion in 1983 compared with $933.7 million in 1982, a gain of 17 percent. Since the start of 1979, the company's revenues increased by nearly 68 percent from $650.7 million. In that same period, net income climbed 116 percent from $36.4 million. Growth was achieved in each year despite periods of serious recession.[37]

The business is diversified geographically and within the communications industry. It has a strong cash flow and a healthy balance sheet. In 1983 its long-term debt was reduced from $153.5 million to $79.6 million, or from 31 percent of total capitalization in 1982 to 16 percent in 1983.

In 1983 the Times Company invested $79.7 million in new plant and equipment, compared with $58.1 million in 1982. In 1984 they expected to invest at about the same level as in 1983.[38]

The significant increase in the operating profit of the newspaper group came from a combination of lower newsprint prices, higher advertising and circulation revenues, and the addition of 12 newspapers acquired late in 1982. The group now consists of *The New York Times* and 29 regional newspapers, diversified both geographically and in size. They range from a 2,500 circulation weekly to a daily of more than 100,000 circulation.[39]

Operating profit in both 1983 and 1982 was affected by special labor charges. In 1983 there was a $2.5 million charge for voluntary early-retirement termination benefits for *Times* stereotypers. And agreement was reached with the newspaper's unions, extending their contracts to March 30, 1987. The extension provided for a $6.5 million wage adjustment retroactive to March 30, 1983. In 1982 there had been a $14.1 million charge for voluntary early-retirement termination benefits for composing-room employees.[40]

Once again in 1983 *The New York Times* set a record for advertising linage, with a total of 104 million lines. It was the second successive year that the paper published over 100 million lines.

Two of the three major advertising categories – retail and national – gained 3.2 and 7.2 percent, respectively. Classified advertising, hurt early in the year by the recession's impact on help-wanted linage, showed a 1.1 percent decline. *The New York Times Magazine* carried 4,196 pages of advertising, a gain of 82 pages over 1982, maintaining its position as no. 2 in ad pages among all U.S. magazines.[41] An advertising rate increase averaging 9 percent was put into effect on January 1, 1984.

Average circulation for the year 1983 rose to 935,000 copies weekdays, a gain of 6,000 copies over the 1982 average. The Sunday average was 1,551,000 copies, a gain of 28,000 copies.

A fourth printing site for the national edition began operation in January 1984 in Walnut Creek, California, near San Francisco, to serve northern California and the Northwest. Operations will begin in the spring at a fifth site, in Austin, Texas. Southern California is served from Torrance, near Los Angeles; the Midwest from Chicago; and the Southeast from Lakeland, Florida. The Boston-Washington corridor is served by editions of the *Times* printed in New York City and Carlstadt, New Jersey.[42]

REGIONAL NEWSPAPERS

With the acquisition of 12 newspapers by the Times Company in seven states in November 1982, the regional newspapers continued their pattern of growth. While advertising volume remained at virtually the same 13-million-inch level, circulation gains outpaced household growth in those communities served by the group.[43]

Times Company newspapers placed either first or second among all newspapers in percentage growth in net paid daily circulation in the states of Alabama, Florida, Kentucky, Louisiana, North Carolina, and Tennessee. For the 18 papers that were in the group for all of 1982 and 1983, weekday circulation was 284,000, up 4.4 percent; Sunday circulation was 251,800, up 5 percent; and the weekly newspapers, with a total circulation of 46,100, were up 5.7 percent. All these gains were well above the national average for newspapers.[44]

Emphasis during the year was on upgrading the facilities of those newspapers that required plant modernization for greater productivity. Efficient new plants, housing the latest color offset presses, will soon be ready for the *Gainesville* (FL) *Sun*; the *Houma* (LA) *Daily Courier*; the *Daily Corinthian* (Corinth, MS); the *Harlan* (KY) *Daily Enterprise*, and the *Sarasota* (FL) *Herald-Tribune*.[45]

The *Herald-Tribune* is the largest newspaper in the regional group. Its new production facility is four miles from the main offices. The plant will receive page images transmitted by high-frequency radio from the composing room, and will have 14 units of Goss Metro offset presses with six color decks.

The headquarters of the regional newspapers moved in 1983 to Atlanta from Lakeland, FL. Early in 1984 a small Florida weekly, the *Zephyrhills News*, was sold.[46]

The New York Times Company continued its expansion into 1985. It reached an agreement in principle to acquire three daily newspapers from the Public Welfare Foundation.

The three newspapers will raise to 20 the number of dailies in the Times regional group based in Atlanta and bring the group's circulation to 510,000. The regional group also owns eight weeklies with a circulation of 58,000.

To be acquired are the morning *Spartanburg* (SC) *Herald-Journal* with 47,000 daily circulation, the evening *Tuscaloosa* (AL) *News* with 30,900 circulation, and the evening *Gadsden* (AL) *Times* with 28,500 circulation.[47]

"Far forward, right-hand page urgently requested" is an expression magazine admen such as *The New York Times Magazine* ad director Philip L. R. DuVal learn to live by. Without such preferential positioning, advertisers might skip issues until they can get it.

But the pace-setting Sunday *New York Times Magazine* is beginning to chip away at this axiom that limits ad sales. It is sprucing up its back-of-the-book fare to appeal to those high-end advertisers that traditionally appear in the up-front pages of the magazine.

Additionally, *The New York Times Magazine* is getting a strong ad infusion from its companion "Part 2" magazine, which will appear 14 times in 1985, and it is encouraging more business from advertisers by opening the pages to furnished inserts, selling second-cover gatefolds, and "zoning" its New York circulation to pull in retail dollars.

This, and more, is moving *The New York Times Magazine* revenues closer to the mass-circulation leaders, *Parade* and *Family Weekly*, in the newspaper-distributed magazine market. *The New York Times Magazine*'s total ad pages remain second only to *Business Week* among all magazines.[48]

The New York Times Company also announced on March 1, 1985, an agreement in principle to acquire *The Santa Rosa Press-Democrat*, a Sonoma County, California, morning daily newspaper with a circulation of 73,000 copies on weekdays and 81,000 copies on Sundays. The acquisition is the Times Company's first on the West Coast.

Financial terms of the agreement, which was disclosed on February 27, were not given, but the Times Company said the deal included the acquisition of *The Healdsburg Tribune*, a twice-weekly newspaper published 16 miles north of Santa Rosa.

Sydney Gruson, vice-chairman of the Times Company, said the company plans a major expansion of the Santa Rosa daily's facilities, adding that the Times Company is enthusiastic about "serving one of the country's most attractive and growing markets." Santa Rosa is about 55 miles north of San Francisco.

The Times Company owns 20 daily and eight weekly newspapers in addition to the flagship New York daily. All except one Maine weekly are in seven Southeastern states. In January 1985 the Times Company agreed to buy three papers in Spartansburg, SC, and Tuscaloosa and Gadsden, AL, from the Public Welfare Foundation in Washington, D.C. Under another recent agreement with the Des Moines Register and Tribune Company, the Times Company will acquire WQAD-TV, which broadcasts to the Quad Cities area of Illinois and Iowa.[49]

The New York Times Company executive staff is listed as follows: Arthur Ochs Sulzberger, chairman; Sydney Gruson, vice-chairman; Walter Mattson, president; David L. Gorham, senior vice-president; Benjamin Handelman, senior vice-president; Michael E. Ryan, senior vice-president; Guy T. Garrett, vice-president; Solomon B. Watson IV, secretary; and Denise K. Fletcher, treasurer.

The Operating Group executives include: William H. Davis, senior vice-president; John D. Pomfret, senior vice-president; Charles B. Brakefield, vice-president; John R. Harrison, vice-president; William T. Kerr, vice-president; and David K. MacDonald, vice-president.

According to Arthur Ochs Sulzberger and Walter E. Mattson in a statement to stockholders, "The New York Times Company is positioned now for further growth through both acquisition and internal development. Our objective continues to be the achievement of an excellent return on investment with quality products. We are confident that this will enhance our Company, reward our shareholders and bring continuing challenge and opportunity to the men and women whose efforts are so essential to our success."[50]

The *Times* has received many awards, including 54 Pulitzer prizes, more than any other newspaper. The *Times* received the first Pulitzer Gold Medal in 1918.

NOTES

1. The credo of *The New York Times*, taken from the salutatory of Adolph S. Ochs, publisher from 1896 to 1935.

2. Meyer Berger, *The Story of The New York Times, 1851-1951*, p. 3. New York: Simon and Schuster, 1951.

3. Ibid.

4. Ibid., pp. 12, 13.

5. Ibid., p. 16.

6. Ibid., p. 32.

7. Ibid., p. 33.

8. Ibid., p. 46.

9. Ibid., p. 67.

10. Ibid., p. 68.

11. Ibid., p. 73.

12. Ibid., pp. 77, 78.

13. Ibid., pp. 79, 80.

14. Elmer Davis, *History of The New York Times, 1851-1921*, pp. 178, 179. New York: The New York Times, 1921.

15. Ibid., p. 180.

16. Ibid., p. 185.

17. Ibid.

18. Ibid., p. 186.

19. Ibid., p. 239.

20. *The New York Times* files.

21. Ibid.

22. David Halberstam, *The Powers That Be*, p. 213. New York: Alfred A. Knopf, 1979.

23. Ibid., p. 214.

24. Ibid., pp. 215, 216.

25. Booz, Allen & Hamilton, Incorporated, report. "*The New York Times*," 1976.

26. Ibid.

27. Ibid.

28. Ibid.

29. Ibid.

30. Ibid.

31. Ibid.

32. Ibid.

33. From Michael Sandretto, *The New York Times* (B), p. 1. Case 9-182-205. Boston, MA: Harvard Business School. Copyright © 1982 by the President and Fellows of Harvard College.

34. Ibid.

35. Ibid.

36. *The New York Times* files.

37. The New York Times Company Annual Report, 1983, p. 2.

38. Ibid., p. 3.

39. Ibid., p. 5.

40. Ibid.

41. Ibid.

42. Ibid., pp. 5, 6.

43. Ibid., p. 6.

44. Ibid.

45. Ibid.

46. Ibid.

47. *Editor & Publisher*, January 19, 1985, p. 24.

48. Craig Endicott, "New York Times Magazine Not Resting on Its Laurels," *Advertising Age*, January 24, 1985, p. 34.

49. *The New York Times*, March 1, 1985, p. 40.

50. Statement to stockholders February 16, 1984, by Arthur Ochs Sulzberger, chairman and chief executive officer, and Walter E. Mattson, president and chief operating officer, the New York Times Company.

11

THE CHICAGO TRIBUNE

The newspaper is an institution developed by modern
civilization to present the news of the day, to foster commerce
and industry, to inform and lead public opinion, and to furnish
that check upon government which no constitution has ever been
able to provide.[1]

Colonel Robert R. McCormick

EARLY HISTORY

From a four-page daily, printed by hand in a rented room in 1847, to
an organization of 13 subsidiary corporations and an investment in seven
partially owned corporations in 1956 – that's the history of the Tribune
company's growth.

The first issue of the *Chicago Tribune* was published June 10, 1847,
as the venture of four men. They were James Kelly and Thomas A.
Stewart, publishers of a weekly literary paper, *Gem of the Prairie*,
launched May 20, 1844, and Col. Joseph K. C. Forrest and John E.
Wheeler.[2]

Medill Joins in 1855

During the *Tribune*'s early years, its management and editorship
changed rapidly. Two weeks after the first issue, Kelly sold out. Forrest
dissolved his connection in September; Wheeler sold his interest in 1851.

Joseph Medill and Dr. Charles Ray arrived in Chicago in the spring of 1855 to negotiate for the purchase of the *Tribune*. On April 27, 1855, an agreement was reached assuring Medill and his associates that they would ultimately gain full ownership of the *Tribune* for $400,000.[3]

It wasn't until June 10, 1855, that a formal announcement of a new ownership arrangement appeared in the newspaper. In the meantime a Timothy Wright had joined the group as a publisher-partner. He was identified as "one of the oldest and most respected citizens of Chicago."[4]

On September 24, 1855, the newspaper was ready to announce new editors, a new Hoe press, and the new "dress" made possible by the fonts of gleaming copper-clad type.[5]

Through the newspapers that it purchased and absorbed, the *Tribune* is the outgrowth of the first publication of any kind printed in Chicago. This was the old *Chicago Democrat*, started November 26, 1833, and absorbed by the *Tribune* in 1861.

Last Merger in 1861

The year 1861 was important for the *Tribune*. It saw the last merger in the newspaper's history. In addition, on February 18 of that year, Gov. Richard Yates approved an act of the Illinois legislature incorporating the Tribune company, the parent organization from which grew subsidiary and affiliated companies.

One of the articles of incorporation reads:

> 3rd. The said Company shall also have the power to manufacture in the city of Chicago and elsewhere, paper . . . and shall have power to purchase and hold so much real estate and water power as may be necessary to carry out the provisions of this Article Third.

Foresighted as were the men who included these powers in the Tribune company incorporation papers, it is unlikely that any of them could have envisioned the vast network of enterprises that came into existence after the newspaper began to exercise its full corporate powers.

For half a century after its incorporation, the *Tribune* continued to buy its newsprint paper in the open market.

Joseph Medill McCormack was born to Robert Sanderson McCormack and Katherine Medill McCormack on May 16, 1877. Another son of the Medill family was Robert Wilson Patterson, Jr., who married Elinor Medill in January 1878. Robert Wilson Patterson, Jr. was born in Chicago on November 30, 1850.[6]

A year after this marriage, on January 6, 1879, the Pattersons became parents of a boy, Joseph Medill Patterson, and on November 7, 1881, Elinor (Cissy) was born.[7]

These latter two people were to be heard from in prominent publishing circles in years to come.

In 1911 it was decided to build a newsprint paper mill. With the incorporation of the Ontario Paper Company on February 29, 1912, the *Tribune* went forward with the construction of its first paper mill at Thorold, Ontario, on the Welland Canal.

Two years later, on January 14, 1914, the Quebec and Ontario Transportation Company was formed to own and operate a fleet of ships for transporting pulpwood logs and finished paper. The same year saw the outbreak of World War I, which temporarily halted the newspaper's expansion program.[8]

NEW YORK NEWS

Shortly after the armistice, Colonel McCormick and Captain Patterson returned from duty overseas with the decision to launch a picture newspaper in New York City. To put this project into effect, the News Syndicate company was incorporated on May 20, 1919, and the *New York News* began publication June 26 of the same year.

To supply the company's expanded needs for newsprint, the Ontario Paper company leased its first timberlands on December 4, 1915, more than 300 square miles on the Rocky River near the mouth of the St. Lawrence River. Here was built Shelter Bay, the *Tribune*'s first timberland town. Logging operations started in 1920.

On May 27, 1920, the firm bought a majority interest in the Franquelin Lumber and Pulpwood Company. This was located on the Franquelin River at Baie des Cedres, about 80 miles southwest of Shelter Bay.[9]

On June 25, 1928, the company acquired all the assets of the Franquelin Lumber and Pulpwood company and absorbed them into the Ontario Paper company.

In January 1923, 2,000 square miles of timberlands on the east branch of the Manicouagan River were leased by the Ontario Paper Company from the Quebec government. Under the terms of the lease a paper mill was to be built near the basin of the Manicouagan or Outardes River.[10]

A small tract between the Manicouagan and Amedee rivers was acquired in 1927, and a tract of 494 square miles along the Amedee, LaChasse, and English rivers was leased in 1929.

Expansion in Chicago continued with the incorporation of Newspaper Readers Agency, Inc., on May 2, 1928. This unit was formed to handle the issuance of Tribune-Federal accident insurance policies offered by the circulation department in connection with home-delivery subscriptions.[11]

$100,000 TOWER CONTEST

On its seventy-fifth birthday, June 10, 1922, the *Tribune* announced a $100,000 contest for the design of an office building to be erected adjacent to the plant it had constructed at 435 N. Michigan Ave., in 1920. Shortly after the winning design for Tribune Tower had been selected, the Chicago Tribune Building corporation was formed September 8, 1923, to take over the development of the great project known today as Tribune Square.

ENTRANCE INTO RADIO

The newspaper's progress in the field of radio was signaled on January 6, 1932. On that date W-G-N, Inc., was formed to take charge of the broadcasting activities launched as early as December 1921, when negotiations were held with KYW, the first Chicago broadcasting station. This led the following month to the inauguration of regular programs of news, stock market reports, and sports summaries, which were furnished by the *Tribune* and broadcast over KYW as the "Tribune-Westinghouse" programs.[12]

For several weeks during the early months of 1924, the *Tribune* operated a station in the Edgewater Beach hotel under the call letters WGN. The station originally had been licensed as WJAZ and at that time was owned by the hotel and the Zenith Radio company.[13]

This is the first recorded use by the *Tribune* of WGN as broadcast call letters. Originally owned by a lake freighter, the call letters were readily relinquished to the *Tribune*.

On June 1, 1924, the *Tribune* severed connections with the Edgewater Beach station and assumed control of station WDAP on the Drake hotel under a lease from the Whitestone company. On July 15, 1924, which is generally accepted as the official birth date of WGN, the call letters of WDAP were changed to WGN. The station was operated under this lease until February 11, 1926, when the *Tribune* purchased the equipment.

WGN-TV went on the air April 5, 1948. On April 16 of the same year, WPIX, Inc., was formed in New York to take over the radio and television operations of the *New York News*.[14]

SALES COMPANIES

On June 14, 1932, the *Tribune* joined with the publishers of other leading Sunday newspapers in the formation of Metropolitan Sunday Newspapers, Inc.

Meanwhile, the increasing popularity throughout the world of comics originated by the *Chicago Tribune* led to the organization on March 27, 1933, of the Chicago Tribune Syndicate and Press Service, Inc. On October 7 of the same year, the name was changed to Chicago Tribune-New York News Syndicate, Inc.[15]

CHICAGO TRIBUNE CHARITIES

Three years later such outstanding box office successes as theGolden Gloves, Music Festival, All-Star football game, and other events sponsored in the public interest were producing such important sums for charity that a separate organization was formed March 19, 1936, to handle the distribution. Thus was created Chicago Tribune Charities, Inc., which through 1955 paid out more than $5 million to charitable organizations benefiting every race and creed through out the Chicago area.[16] A similar organization, the News Welfare association, was formed by the *New York News* on July 27, 1937.

On November 30, 1936, with the *New York News* and the *Philadelphia Inquirer*, the *Tribune* was active in forming Three Markets Group, Inc., organized to promote the sale of advertising in the roto picture sections of the three newspapers on a combination basis.

Events of the next two years opened the second great era in the company's paper-producing and timberland operations. Construction of a new paper mill began at Baie Comeau in April 1936. On February 19, 1937, the Baie Comeau Company was incorporated to take charge of housing and otherwise care for the needs of the army of workers who carved out of the wilderness an entire new community and built in it the *Tribune*'s second paper mill.

To own and operate the mill, the Quebec North Shore Paper Company, Ltd., was incorporated July 8, 1938.[17]

A TRANSPORTATION COMPANY

This new expansion created the need for additional facilities to transport the finished paper from Baie Comeau to the warehouses of the *New York News* in New York. To provide these facilities, a transportation company was acquired on May 17, 1940. Originally called the Colabee Steamship company, later the Michigan Atlantic corporation, the name was changed to the Illinois Atlantic corporation on April 7, 1942.

The Ontario Paper company increased its holdings in 1937 by acquiring 781 square miles of timber on the Black River near Heron Bay, Ontario, on the northern shore of Lake Superior. A 250-foot wharf, town, power plant, barking mill, and flume were completed in 1939.[18]

LEASING ADDITIONAL LIMITS

Seven years later the company leased an additional 100 square miles in the Black River section and in 1948 by transference of a lease acquired 546 square miles on the nearby Little Pic River.

When the new mill at Baie Comeau increased the demand for the various ingredients of paper, Marlhill Mines, Ltd., was incorporated January 15, 1942, to provide calcium carbonate, a chemical used as a filler in paper manufacture.

New timber limits were added by the Ontario Paper company in 1947 with the purchase of 65,000 acres on Manitoulin and Cockburn islands in the northern part of Lake Huron. Later purchases brought these holdings to 78,000 acres.[19]

The year 1949 saw further important progress with the formation of the Manicouagan Power Company on January 27. To assure a power reserve to meet the increasing demands of the Baie Comeau mill and community, this new company launched a $15 million hydroelectric project. The first step in this project was the building of the McCormick Dam, a gigantic engineering feat that was completed April 15, 1952.

The Quebec North Shore Paper company also operates a two-generator 70,000 horsepower hydroelectric plant on the Outardes River, a few miles west of the Manicouagan.

In 1951 the Ontario Paper Company again added to its reserves by obtaining a 21-year concession on a tract of 612 square miles of timberland near Lac Seul, about 225 miles north of Port Arthur, Ontario. At the same time, 608 square miles of timber adjoining this area was reserved for the company.

COLONEL ROBERT R. McCORMICK

Colonel Robert R. McCormick's first active contact with the *Tribune* began on February 15, 1909, when he became treasurer of the Tribune Company. At this time he was more actively engaged in the political phase of his career, being president of the Sanitary District Board, a post he held from 1905 to 1910.

One day in April 1910, Colonel McCormick received a phone call informing him of the death of Robert W. Patterson. Upon arrival at Mr. Patterson's office, he experienced another shock. He discovered that a group of stockholders were meeting there for the purpose of accepting an offer from Victor Lawson, publisher of the *Chicago Daily News* and the *Chicago Record-Herald*, to purchase the *Tribune*. Lawson's offer, made on the basis of ten times the *Tribune*'s annual earnings, figured somewhere between $6.25 and $8.14 million.[20]

As the Colonel stated years later in his memoirs, "the idea of selling the *Tribune* appalled me." Following his whole-hearted disapproval of the idea of selling the *Tribune* to Lawson, or to anyone else, the stockholders originally in favor of accepting the offer changed their minds and agreed to reject it. They laid down one condition, however. They would oppose the sale only if the Colonel "would enter actively into the management of the *Tribune*."

The Colonel's agreement to become continuously active in the management of the *Tribune* began with his subsequent notification of Lawson that the *Tribune* would not be sold. His managerial association with the *Tribune* became permanent on March 1, 1911, when he was elected president of the Tribune Company.[21]

Circulation

It is interesting to note both the circulation and advertising linage of Chicago newspapers in 1911 when Colonel McCormick was elected president of the Tribune Company:[22]

Chicago Newspaper Circulation, 1911

Tribune, daily	241,075
Tribune, Sunday	352,328
News	322,838
Journal	99,009 [a]
Post	51,852 [a]
American	357,341
Examiner, daily	208,924
Examiner, Sunday	522,342
Record-Herald, daily	200,132
Record-Herald, Sunday	213,690
Inter-Ocean, daily	70,500 [b]
Inter-Ocean, Sunday	110,000 [b]

[a]Circulation for 1912; no record for 1911.
[b]Circulation for 1910; no record for 1911.

Source: Chicago Tribune Company files.

Chicago Newspapers' Total Advertising Linage in 1911

	Daily	*Sunday*	*Total*
Tribune	6,951,939	4,472,826	11,424,765
Record-Herald	4,464,831	2,879,373	7,344,204
Inter-Ocean	2,302,194	1,502,754	3,804,948
Examiner	4,373,931	3,024,525	7,398,456
News	9,218,874		
American	3,736,584		
Post	2,736,584		
Journal	4,081,707		

Note: Total advertising linage for all seven Chicago newspapers was 49,792,926.
Source: Chicago Tribune Company files.

One of the outstanding achievements in Colonel McCormick's career had its inception shortly after he became president of the Tribune Company in March 1911. Because of his conviction that the *Tribune* should manufacture its own newsprint paper, a vast auxiliary enterprise came into existence. Later the manufacture of newsprint for the *Chicago Tribune* and the *New York News* used the full capacity of two great paper mills producing more than 350,000 tons of paper annually. Pulpwood for the mills comes from timberlands in the provinces of Quebec and Ontario, covering more than 7,500 square miles, an area greater than that of the combined states of Connecticut and Delaware. A fleet of ships, diesel and steam powered, carries newsprint from the mills to the *Tribune* and the *New York News*.

Construction of the *Tribune*'s first paper mill, the one at Thorold on the Welland Canal, began in 1912. It began turning out newsprint in September 1913. By the end of the year it had produced 5,718 tons of paper. Its total for 1914 was 31,704 tons. Later its annual production was well in excess of 175,000 tons.[23]

The final decision to start the *New York News* came one day during World War I, on the Marne battlefield as Colonel McCormick and his cousin, Captain Joseph Medill Patterson, sat on the only available spot higher than the ground, a manure pile. The idea for starting the *News* came from observation of the highly successful London newspaper, the *Daily Mail*, which devoted a far larger percentage of its space to printing pictures than had ever before been done by a newspaper.[24]

The first issue of the *New York News* appeared on June 26, 1919. It printed 150,000 copies all of which were sold before the day's end. However, a slump soon set in after this seemingly auspicious opening. By August, the *News'* circulation had reached its all-time low with a circulation of 26,635. That was the turning point. Circulation began a continuous upward trend. By January 1920, it was 141,238 copies. In January of the following year the figure was close to half a million. Today the *News'* daily circulation is around 1.5 million and its Sunday circulation approximately 2 million.[25]

In 1914 Colonel McCormick was called to an active executive position in the *Tribune* when he and his cousin, Captain Joseph Medill Patterson, jointly assumed the posts of editor and publisher. With the founding of the *Tribune*'s subsidiary, the *New York News*, in 1919, and Captain Patterson's association with the new newspaper as editor and publisher, more and more of the task of running the *Tribune* devolved to

McCormick. In 1925 he became the *Tribune*'s sole editor and publisher.[26]

Following Captain Patterson's death in May 1946, Colonel McCormick became chairman of the board and vice-president of the News-Syndicate Co., Inc., the Tribune Company subsidiary that controls the *New York News*. He was also elected chairman of the Syndicate, Inc., which sells comics and features to newspapers in the United States and abroad.[27]

The immense growth of color printing, not only in the *Chicago Tribune* but in newspapers generally, can be attributed largely to Colonel McCormick's foresight and to his unremitting efforts to bring about this advance in newspaper production. In 1920 he ordered the construction of an experimental press from which was eventually evolved the method of colorotogravure printing introduced by the *Tribune* in 1922. The greatest single impetus given to the now widespread use of newsprint color printing by U.S. newspapers came from its adoption by the *Tribune* in 1926.[28]

In conferring an honorary Doctorate of Laws on Colonel McCormick in 1935, Colby College made note of his chairmanship of the Freedom of the Press Committee of the American Newspaper Publishers Association by stating that in such capacity he had "rendered eminent service in guarding that freedom against inroad, qualification or abridgement."

When in 1947 Northwestern University bestowed the degree of LL.D. on the *Tribune*'s publisher, the citation referred to him as "a generous friend of Northwestern whose imagination and foresight were responsible for the establishment of the Medill School of Journalism, and whose sincere, courageous and long continued efforts to preserve freedom of the press and the liberties of the people have contributed fundamentally to the present and future welfare of the nation."[29]

The news of Colonel McCormick's death on April 1, 1955, resulted in a flood of tributes to him from every section of U.S. society and from many foreign lands. The publishers of Chicago's three other daily newspapers were among the many who expressed the feelings of leading U.S. newspapermen.

Marshall Field, Jr., publisher of the *Chicago Sun-Times*, said, "Colonel McCormick was a great publisher and a great gentleman. Chicago will miss him very much."[30]

John S. Knight, publisher of the *Chicago Daily News*, said, "The Colonel will be missed by friend and foe alike. He has been a colorful and significant figure in journalism for nearly half a century."

Stuart List, publisher of the *Chicago American,* said: "I had great respect for Colonel McCormick as an American, as a newspaper man, and as a citizen."

Typical of the hundreds of tributes from newspapers all over the United States was an article in *The New York Times* which, in speaking of McCormick's relations to the *Chicago Tribune,* said: "He boldly stamped it with his own likeness, impregnated it with his own vitality and virtuosity, and through it, made his dynamic impact felt on American life. He was one of America's last exemplars among publishers of the era of personal journalism."[31]

CHICAGO TRIBUNE MAGAZINE

For several years now the *Tribune Magazine* has functioned as a general-interest publication within a Sunday newspaper increasingly made up of special-interest sections. In the selection of subjects it has operated within no fixed boundaries. However, like the rest of the *Tribune,* its principal focus has been on people, places, and events throughout the greater Chicago area.

This does not mean that the magazine has not roamed widely outside Illinois in search of material. But it has been, above all, a Midwestern publication addressing matters of greatest interest to its Midwestern audience.

Its principal mission has been to entertain. But at times it has also addressed serious subjects to help readers more clearly understand the complex world around us.[32]

Point of View

What we've attempted to create and maintain in our pages is a personality – a distinct point of view, a consistent tone of voice, and a willingness to do the unexpected. We've tried to be "smart" in both senses of the word: intelligent and informed; sassy (at times) and irreverent. We've also worked to demonstrate a sense of humor – in our choice of cover artwork, cover type, readouts, headlines, and inside illustrations.

In short, we've sought to convey a view of the world that is sophisticated and at the same time sufficiently down-to-earth to avoid alienating our more traditional readers.

Use of Color

Like other roto publications, the magazine's greatest strength is its high-quality color reproduction; no other section of the newspaper can display color photos and illustrations with the same impact. Making the most of this unique advantage has been another of our goals. First, we've tried to showcase in color photos the best material from local art exhibits. We've focused in recent months on shows at the Museum of Science and Industry (Treasures of Tiffany); the Field Museum (artifacts of the Maritime Indians); Chicago Historical Society (Folk Art of Illinois); and the Art Institute of Chicago (Vatican Collections; Photographs of the Midwestern Prairie).[33]

Graphic Design

Every successful periodical in America – be it *Time, New York, Foreign Affairs* or *Consumer Reports* – has a special "look" to it, a graphic style that sets it apart. In 1982, to achieve to look of our own, the *Tribune Magazine* underwent a facelift. A simple, straight-forward, no-frills design format was introduced. Several headline faces – Cable Heavy, Aachen Bold, Helvetica Black – were selected for regular use in our pages.[34]

THE *TRIBUNE* TODAY

Today the Tribune Company is a diversified communications company with assets of $1.6 billion in newspaper publishing, broadcasting and entertainment, cable television, and newsprint forest products.[35]

The principal newspapers are in Chicago; New York; Fort Lauderdale and Orlando, Florida; and in Los Angeles, Palo Alto, and Escondido, California.[36]

In 1983, after 136 years of private ownership, the company and selling shareholders made the first public offering of stock (valued at $206 million), the largest initial public offering by an industrial company in a quarter-century.[37]

After a year as a public concern the Tribune Company is prospering. The company reported its best-ever third quarter in 1984: profits were $27.9 million, up 123 percent from a year earlier.[38]

However, Stanton R. Cook, the Chicago-based company's 59-year-old chairman and chief executive officer acknowledges the company has a long way to go before it reaches the goal he has set for it – an 18 percent return on equity.[39]

"I think 18 percent is a realizable goal," Mr. Cook said in his plush, pecan-paneled office, which once belonged to Col. Robert McCormick, the autocratic, conservative publisher who died in 1955. "We've made some important progress. I can't tell exactly when we'll hit that goal, but I hope to see it soon."[40]

For the 20 years after the Colonel's death, a group of trustees ran the company without much dynamism or direction. Mr. Cook took over in 1975, and Wall Street analysts praise him for bringing modern management to the company.[41]

The Tribune Company's eight dailies, including three small ones in California, make it the fourth-largest company in terms of daily newspaper circulation. Its television properties – including WPIX in New York and stations in Chicago, Denver, Atlanta, and New Orleans – make it the fifth-largest broadcasting group in terms of potential audience.[42]

Mr. Cook says that, for a media company as broadly based as the Tribune Company, the economic recovery is a powerful engine for increased earnings. Its newspapers' retail advertising revenues jumped 11 percent in 1983, and classified revenues rose 16 percent. Net income for the first nine months of 1984 was $67.1 million, up 90 percent from the comparable period a year ago and just slightly below the $69.3 million for all of 1983. Revenues totaled $1.29 billion in the first nine months of 1983, up 13 percent from the comparable period a year ago, and sales were $1.59 billion in 1983.

As a result of this earnings jump, Tribune stock, which sold for $26.75 a share in its $125 million public offering in October 1983, rose to $33 a share in November 1984.[43]

Net income of the Tribune Company in 1984 rose to a record $103 million, up 49 percent from $69.3 million a year earlier. Earnings per share increased 35 percent to a record $2.55 from $1.89. Revenues were up 13 percent to $1.79 billion from $1.59 billion last year.

Leading contributors to 1984's record results were record operating profits among newspaper and broadcasting groups, the turnaround in newsprint and forest products operations in Canada, and lower interest expense.[44]

In the fourth quarter ended December 30, net income grew 6 percent to $36 million from $34 million while earnings per share rose to $.89, a

5 percent increase over 1983. Revenues in the quarter were $501.4 million, up 14 percent from $438.5 million last year.[45]

Company newspapers in Chicago, Fort Lauderdale, Orlando, Los Angeles, and Escondido each reported record revenues and operating profits for the year with earnings gains averaging more than 35 percent. However, profit growth for the group was held down by relocation, circulation, and buyout costs at the *New York Daily News*; employee termination expenses at the *Peninsula Times Tribune* in Palo Alto; and relocation and development costs at Tribune Media Services.[46]

NOTES

1. Colonel Robert R. McCormick, former editor and publisher of the *Chicago Tribune*, address before the Chicago Church Federation, Chicago, IL, October 1924.
2. *Chicago Tribune* files.
3. Lloyd Wendt, *Chicago Tribune*, pp. 59, 62. Chicago: Rand McNally & Company, 1979.
4. Ibid., p. 63.
5. Ibid., p. 64.
6. Wendt, *Tribune*, p. 278.
7. Ibid., p. 279.
8. *Chicago Tribune*, May 1956, p. 5.
9. Ibid.
10. Ibid.
11. Ibid.
12. Ibid.
13. Ibid.
14. Ibid., p. 12.
15. Ibid.
16. Ibid.
17. Ibid.
18. Ibid.
19. Ibid.
20. Chicago Tribune Company files.
21. Ibid.
22. Ibid.
23. Ibid.
24. Ibid.
25. Ibid.
26. Chicago Tribune Company files.
27. Ibid.
28. Ibid.
29. Ibid.
30. Ibid.
31. Ibid.

32.   John Twohey, editor, the *Chicago Tribune Magazine,* "Chicago Tribune Magazine, Sophisticated, Yet Down-to-Earth." A Report on Sunday Magazines, Associated Press Managing Editors, Changing Newspapers Committee, Spring 1983, p. 9.

33.   Ibid.

34.   Ibid.

35.   Annual Report, Tribune Company, 1983, p. 1.

36.   Ibid.

37.   Ibid., p. 2.

38.   Steven Greenhouse, "The Prospering Tribune Company," *The New York Times,* November 7, 1984, p. 33.

39.   Ibid.

40.   Ibid., p. 37.

41.   Ibid.

42.   Ibid.

43.   Ibid.

44.   A progress report from the Tribune Company, 1984, p. 1.

45.   Ibid.

46.   Ibid.

12

EPILOGUE

OVERVIEW

A daily newspaper is a transitory thing, a "first rough draft of history" as Philip Graham remarked. The study of the practice of newspaper management is a stimulating and worthwhile endeavor for anyone interested in reading newspapers, purchasing paid advertising space therein, or choosing the newspaper industry as a career.

From the first newspaper published in the United States, Benjamin Harris' *Publick Occurrences Both Foreign and Domestick*, newspapers have functioned as a unique and vital force in the daily lives of millions of Americans.

Following a study of early newspapers the author stressed the importance of the circulation operation and its contribution to the profit picture. In recent years the circulation directors of daily newspapers are taking their rightful place in the newspaper executive suite.

Managing as an art was then defined, and the structure of eight important departments was described in detail. Personal interviews and quotations from leading newspaper publishers were outlined, presenting a rare opportunity to hear from executives charged with meeting a weekly payroll.

"Nothing ever happens until somebody sells something." This adage is certainly applicable to the newspaper business. Newspaper advertising is the life blood of the industry and again we have the advantage of a personal interview with one of the country's top newspaper advertising and marketing executives.

The book also outlined the functions and responsibilities of the newspaper industry's leading associations, including the American Newspaper Publishers Association, with its 1,384 members founded in 1887, the important Newspaper Advertising Bureau, the International Newspaper Advertising and Marketing Executives Association, and the International Circulation Managers Association.

A discussion of new developments in the newspaper industry would not be complete without a thorough analysis of *USA TODAY* starting with its beginning in September 1982. Keith Rupert Murdock's recent exploits in the newspaper world were also covered, including his theory of management.

The book concentrated in the later chapters on a case history analysis of four leading daily newspapers in major markets. The newspapers chosen are all well-managed enterprises, and most successful from both an editorial and business standpoint. They are the *Los Angeles Times*, *The Washington Post*, *The New York Times*, and the *Chicago Tribune*.

According to James Hoge, chairman, CEO, New York News, Inc.:

If newspapers are to claim for themselves a greater role in educating and informing, they must look to their own ability and credibility while doing so. The consumers movement of the last two decades is still with us and it is indeed in a vacuum. The seeds of distrust in the marketplace have been sung by the careless manufacturer, or the unscrupulous vendor, and the entire business world is left to reap the whirlwind of investigative scrutiny and legislation which followed.

Now it is the standard practice of practically every newspaper to screen and evaluate advertising before it is accepted. The degree to which it is examined to prove its inaccuracy is necessarily a function of time and staffing. However, there is a generally recognized agreement that newspapers have an obligation to take some steps to protect their readers from those who would prey on them. These efforts are a result of concern of the newspapers' three greatest assets; its readers, its advertisers and its credibility. Obviously all three interact with misleading advertising. Loss of faith in the advertising of the newspaper reduces its worth to both the reader and to the advertiser. A sort of Grecian's law then applies in that good advertising that is truthful advertising is driven out of the newspaper by untruthful or bad advertising. The result of course is the gradual withering of the economic life line and the demise of the newspaper.

Speaking of controls involving marketing of goods and services is difficult enough, but it is possible through constant vigilance, but a newspaper is also to the itinerant reader a marketplace for ideas and opinions and these are not so easily monitored or evaluated. Indeed the very process for screening which is acceptable for advertising, if not desirable, is onerous, and an apt one when applied to news coverage and editorial views.[1]

WEEKLY NEWSPAPERS

Although large daily newspapers are emphasized throughout this book, business and journalism students should realize that there are also stimulating and profitable opportunities in smaller community daily newspapers and in hometown weekly newspapers.

According to the National Newspaper Association there are 7,101 weekly hometown newspapers in the United States, located in every state in the union. The association is located in Washington, D.C., and is directed by Melvin Street, executive vice-president. He reports to a ten-member board of directors located in ten strategic regional locations.

National advertising for the weekly newspaper is sold by American Newspaper Representatives, Inc., a wholly-owned subsidary of the Association. According to this advertising sales representative organization, "hometown" newspapers are unique, unusual – and powerful. The dealers are local, the customers are local, the sales are local, and hometown newspapers are the only medium that give local saturation coverage.

The 41 million household market represents more sales – and more sales potential – of almost everything. The markets saturated by hometown newspapers range from the wealthiest suburbs, to new suburbs of prosperous, young, growing households, to the small-town market that is the heart of America. Comprising 44 percent of the U.S. households, these markets represent one-half of the U.S. income.[2]

COMMUNITY DAILY NEWSPAPERS

Community or small-town daily newspapers are also a vital newspaper force in this country, and offer important career opportunities.

Stephen W. Ryder, vice-president of Ottaway Newspapers, Inc., has the following viewpoints on the subject, expressed during a personal interview:

Four out of every five daily newspapers in this country have circulations under 50,000. Frequently, they cover and penetrate their markets more effectively than the big, metropolitan papers do.

Yet, many new journalism graduates who are business management oriented, seem mesmerized by size. Behind the initial lure of the "Top 20," major market papers too often have been faced with problems of diminishing circulation, lost advertising, skyrocketing costs, outdated equipment and eroding reader confidence.

Meanwhile, many of the nation's 1,450 smaller dailies have quietly earned the respect of their communities and a reputation for excellence. Circulations grow with growing markets, relationships with readers improve and advertisers get results.

This is the "secret" I want to share with new journalism graduates: if you want to show your skills, be appreciated and have an opportunity to grow, consider America's local newspapers, the "under 50,000" ones. You may be surprised, even thrilled and rewarded with an unusually satisfying career opportunity.

There's a tremendous sense of achievement when you help develop a newspaper's quality. It can become a professional "calling" with an idealism of the ordination of a clergyman or accreditation of a physician. In a newsroom of 40 to 50 people, or as part of a business, advertising or marketing team of 10 to 20, you are a key person. Your effort makes a difference.

But you must like action and inter-action. Local newspapers are alive with tragedies and triumphs, people and problems, close to home. Personal, face-to-face relationships are the style for staffers in all departments.

Day-by-day, your newspaper grows as you perform. When management and staff are inspired, a quality begins to emerge that enhances the newspaper in the eyes of its readers. In this pursuit of improvement and even excellence, news clout is strengthened, results increase for advertisers, revenues grow . . . providing the income to attract and develop better employees at improved pay and benefits, buy newer equipment to achieve an even better newspaper. And you are a vital part of this spiral to excellence.

Proximity to readers imposes responsibility. Publisher or printer, writer or account manager, each edition is highly visible, mistakes and all. One develops courtesy and humility as well as courage when reporting necessary but perhaps uncomfortable facts about a neighbor. An Oregon publisher put it this way: "In local newspapers, the distance between theory and practice is only an arm's length."

College journalism graduates with business management emphasis may qualify at local newspapers in display, telemarketing and classified advertising departments, in circulation sales development, marketing and research, or the business and controller's office. Increasingly, regular readership and marketing surveys are being locally conducted to assist in action, long range and strategic planning.

Mid-market and smaller newspapers, whether individually or group-owned, often invest heavily in training and development of their staffers. Promotion from within is one of the rewards for performance. Inter-newspaper training is typical in group operations, positioning ambitious people on management training plans that can lead to department management and executive status. Advancement and new opportunities develop, perhaps at various locations, while increased pay and plus benefits continue without the losses from changing employers.

Graduates face a decision. If they wish to work and live in places where they can be involved with leadership people of business, government, schools, civic affairs and the like, the kind of communities that offer a sense of worth and place for individuals and families, these newspapers should be considered. If being a part of a significant and useful profession where one can make a difference, gaining both satisfaction and suitable pay, benefits and peace-of-mind and if one seeks responsibility and appreciation, as well as response from his or her efforts, then the challenge of local newspapering may be the answer.

More and more, qualified graduates are competing for this rewarding journalistic lifestyle in the real worlds of community and mid-market America.[3]

IMPLICATIONS FOR BUSINESS SCHOOL AND JOURNALISM SCHOOL STUDENTS

Given the fact that there is a paucity of business and management courses offered on a regular basis at most journalism schools, this book provides clues to some interesting directions to explore. First, as a minihistory of the origins, growth, decline, and success of important newspapers, it could serve as a point of departure for business journalism students to develop a clearer understanding of both the power and the perishability of the newspaper product; to recognize the fact that editorial excellence alone is not sufficient for a publication's health or survival; and that well-managed, innovative business management is an essential concomitant to its success.

More specifically, journalism students could benefit from a study of the business techniques of eighteenth- and nineteenth-century newspaper publishers. As Peter F. Drucker stated, "There is only one valid definition of business purpose: to create a customer."[4] A study of how customers were created in those early days, and for what purposes, could lead students to an analysis of current methods and purposes of attracting customers to newspapers and to a study of trends that might affect their approach to the future.

Similarly, a comparison of newspaper management diversification techniques could provide student insight into the need for a corporate structure that includes properties other than a single newspaper to provide financial resources sufficient to subsidize a newspaper over a difficult period, whether it be the result of editorial faltering, unanticipated business competition, or unfortunate, but correctable, marketing decisions.

The early history of the business processes of newspapers around the turn of the century indicated the necessity for a thorough knowledge of management techniques. The early publishers attempted to act as editors as well as publishers of their newspapers, and this resulted in failures and a meager income for many who survived. There was no national advertising and the newspapers' income was confined to the subscription or direct-sale price. Early newspaper entrepreneurs attempted to carry out all operations individually without delegating authority. Those managers diffused their talents by engaging in disparate projects in order to extend their fortunes.

A study of the major innovations and improved management techniques adopted by the selected newspapers in this book could provide students, aspiring to careers in business journalism, with case studies of actual problem-solving approaches which, successful then, suggest exploration of courses of action germane to today's situations.

Implicit in the analysis of the four newspapers researched as case studies are a number of cogent parallels in their histories and the need for thorough business management training and education. There is evidence throughout the book that newspapers derived their revenue from two income streams – circulation and advertising. In the early days, without national advertising, circulation accounted for the major share of income proportion. After 1900, when national advertising began, newspapers thrived on this revenue, and circulation pricing decreased to a point where publishers were selling at less than cost.

We, however, should be aware that the pendulum swung back and that modern newspaper publishers concentrated on retail or local advertising and on structuring their circulation operation to the point where its profitability is becoming closer to that of advertising. The above is another example of the need for management dexterity and awareness in business journalism training.

The personal characteristics of the leading publishers reported on in the study are worthy of exploration. As historian Allan Nevins wrote, business cannot be interpreted solely by statistics of prices and profits. These newspaper publishing executives were described in detail in many instances, and students may profit by a scrutiny of both their laudable and uncommendable characteristics.

Throughout the book the need for marketing skills in newspaper publishing is apparent. The successful newspapers were considered by their publishers as an entity, calling for skills in proper distribution, timely sales promotion, correct pricing, dynamic packaging, adequate consumer awareness through advertising, and sound salesmanship. All of these functions are worthy of consideration as bases for business management journalism courses.

Most journalism schools today still concern themselves primarily with preparing students to be editorial journalists. They are not preparing them as business managers. Yet, this research sharply confirms the importance of sound business management in every phase of journalistic endeavor to the success of a newspaper. It is increasingly clear that management and its skills are not the responsibility of those on the business side alone. Artists and designers, editors and writers must join publishers and other top management executives in mastering the techniques of management and applying them to the discipline they direct. An investigation into the possible administration prerequisites in the curricula of journalism and business schools could result in the development of programs of study of more immediate and practical value to journalism students. Future journalists who understand and appreciate the principles of newspaper economics, as well as those of editorial concept and execution, would be in better positions to understand and further the importance of newspapers in the total communications process.

NOTES

1. James Hoge, chairman, CEO, New York News, Inc., publisher *New York Daily News*, address delivered to the 1984 General Conference of the Audit Bureau of Circulations, Royal York Hotel, Toronto, Ontario, October 31, 1984.

2. 1984 National Directory of Weekly Newspapers, published by American Newspaper Representatives, Inc.

3. Personal interview with Stephen W. Ryder, vice-president, Ottaway Newspapers, Inc., Tempe, Arizona, March 29, 1985.

4. Peter F. Drucker, *Management*, p. 61. New York: Harper & Row, 1974.

GLOSSARY OF
NEWSPAPER TERMS —————————

The effectiveness of ABC standards depends on a common understanding of terms used in those standards.

Through its bylaws and rules and through its practices, the Audit Bureau has established definitions for many of the terms used in circulation accounting – from such slang as "eat" papers to the more technical "split-run."

The following glossary is provided to assist the reader in better understanding terms used in ABC newspaper Audit Reports and Publisher's Statements:

advertised price The basic price of publication.

advertisers' copies Copies of a publication given to advertisers in the publication (one copy to each advertiser) for checking their advertisements.

advertising agencies' copies Copies of a publication given to advertising agencies for the purpose of checking advertisements placed by such agencies.

all other A phrase used specifically in newspaper reports to designate all circulation not included in city and retail trading zones or primary market area.

arrears Subscribers retained on active subscription list after expiration.

association subscription Subscription received as part of membership in an association.

audit Examination of a publisher's records and corroborative data in order to check for correctness in the Publisher's Statements covering the period audited.

Audit Report Official document issued by the Audit Bureau of Circulations (ABC), detailing its findings as the result of audit. (On white paper to differentiate it from Publisher's Statements.)

average paid Average paid circulation of all the issues arrived at by dividing the total paid circulation of all the issues during the period by the total number of issues.

back copies An issue of a publication is considered to be a back copy immediately upon the appearance for sale of the next issue.

basic prices The price at which the publication may be purchased by anyone, without limitation, for a definite duration, in contrast to a special price for a limited period or to a limited class or under limited conditions.

Blue Book A semiannual volume of released ABC Publisher's Statements.

bulk sales Quantity sales of copies of a single issue or subscriptions of two or more consecutive issues to one purchaser.

business publication A publication dealing with management, manufacturing, sales, or operation of industries or some specific industry, occupation, or profession, published to interest and assist persons actively engaged in the field it covers.

call-at-office subscribers Subscribers who obtain their copies at office of publication.

carrier Individual engaged in delivery of newspapers.

carrier delivery by independent carriers filing lists System of newspaper operation by which accounts with subscribers are kept and collections are made by the carrier, who furnishes a list of such subscribers to publisher periodically.

carrier delivery office collect system System of newspaper operation by which accounts with subscribers are kept by the newspaper and collections are made by the paper's own employees or designated agents.

carrier, independent One who carries or delivers newspapers to subscribers but who keeps their own list of such subscribers and makes collections on their own account.

checking copy Copy of a publication sent to an advertiser or an advertising agency for verification of advertising insertion.

clubs Two or more subscriptions to the same publication obtained by solicitors, not part of publisher's organization, under plan of offering specific reward for sending in a specific number of subscriptions.

combination sale Subscriptions to two or more different publications sold at a special combination price.

complimentary copies Copies given as a courtesy.

contest Competition among subscription solicitors or among carriers and dealers or among readers or prospective readers of a publication for a prize of money or other valuable consideration.

contest popularity Competition to determine most popular individual in some particular profession, vocation, or social position, decided by the greatest number of votes received, based on coupons clipped from the publication.

correspondents' copies Copies of a publication given to correspondents of the paper, reporters, and editorial writers.

counter sales Newspapers sold over publisher's counter to individual purchasers. If sold in quantities of 11 or more, such copies are allocated to bulk sales.

credit subscription A subscription for which payment is not made at time of order.

distribution The total number of copies distributed per issue whether paid, non-paid, or unpaid.

distributor A general term applied to carriers, dealers, street vendors and all others who sell publications as a vocation or part of their vocation.

draw The number of copies of a publication charged to dealer, carrier, or other distributor.

"eat" papers To accept and pay for more copies than one has customers.

edition All copies of a portion of the total distribution of an issue of a newspaper or periodical, other than replate or split-run, in which the editorial and/or advertising content has been changed. *See also* replate; split-run.

employees' copies Copies given to employees.

exchanges Free copies sent by a publication to other publications in mutual courtesy.

expiration End of period for which subscription was paid.

extension Extending of a subscription beyond its original expiration date because of lowering of subscription price or reducing the frequency of issue.

extra Edition of a newspaper other than those issued regularly each day.

hotel copies Copies purchased by a hotel or motel and distributed free to guests. Copies similarly distributed by restaurants, clubs, and transportation companies are included in the same designation. They are included in bulk sales regardless of number.

individual mail subscription Individual subscription served by mail and qualifying as paid.

mail subscription Order received by mail directly from a subscriber.
motor route Delivery of single copies by means of motor transport to subscribers in rural or sparsely settled areas outside a city, town, or other incorporated area.

net press run Total of copies printed suitable for distribution.
news agent A distributor of newspapers or periodicals at wholesale.
newsdealer A merchant with fixed place of doing business who buys newspapers or periodicals to sell again at retail.
newspaper supplement A compilation of syndicated and/or locally edited features, news items, or editorial comment and advertising distributed with no represented or advertised value, as a separate part or section of a newspaper.
nonreturnable Not subject to credit on being returned. A sales plan in which dealers or other distributors purchase their copies with the understanding that they must pay for all copies purchased whether they sell them or not.

premium Anything, except periodicals, offered to a subscriber, either free or at a price, with a subscription, either direct, or by agent.
publisher's interim statement Statement of publisher, made to ABC at the publisher's option and issued unaudited (but subject to audit) by the Bureau.
Publisher's Statement Statement of circulation data made to ABC by a publisher member of the Bureau and issued unaudited (but subject to audit) by the Bureau.

rack sales Sales of newspapers from racks or boxes, placed on street corners or other convenient points, with the customer depositing coin in payment in a box provided for the purpose. Same as "box" or "honor box" sales.

reduced prices Subscriptions or single copies sold at prices less than the basic price.

replate A change of one or more pages during the printing of an edition or issue of a publication. This procedure generally serves the purpose of adding late news items or of correcting an error in the original copy.

returnable Copies of publications sold to distributors under agreement to take back those unsold. Fully returnable means that all copies sold to any and all distributors may be returned if unsold. Limited returnable is used in two senses. First, when a part of the distribution is sold on a returnable basis and part on a nonreturnable basis; second, when distributors are allowed the return privilege but only of a certain percentage of the quantity purchased.

returns Copies returned to publisher by dealer or other distributor for credit. Frequently, to save transportation charges, complete copies are not returned but only paper headings or covers.

sample copies Copies distributed free to prospective subscribers or prospective advertisers. Copies delivered as part of a contractual arrangement shall not be counted as sample copies.

sheet-writer Name applied to a class of subscription salespeople who receive high percentage of subscription price, often 100 percent, and sometimes a bonus. While subscriptions obtained by a sheet-writer are often fully paid by subscribers, the conditions under which they work sometimes result in their accepting less than the subscription price. Frequently they work on a contract which requires them to turn in a certain quota per day, which induces them at times to send in names of persons who have not subscribed. Sometimes they handle several publications, some of which they offer free in order to get a subscription for a publication on which they get a bonus.

short-term subscription Subscription for less than a year.

special six-month statement A statement issued by the Bureau instead of Publisher's Statement. It is based on data already audited.

split period audit Audit covering a period other than that covered by the regular Publisher's Statement period.

split-run The insertion or substitution of different advertising content for a portion of the distribution of an edition or of an issue for either a newspaper or periodical.

sponsored subscriptions Subscriptions obtained through cooperation between publisher and an organized local civic or charitable organization, members of schools, churches, fraternal or similar organizations, with the publisher donating a portion of the subscription price to the organization involved.

street sales Newspapers sold by individuals on the street or through racks, as distinguished from those sold by dealers with permanent shops or by a carrier with a regular list of customers.

street vendors Sellers of newspapers on streets.

subscription agency An individual, firm, or corporation obtaining subscriptions for two or more publications.

subscription salespeople's copies Copies of a publication carried by subscription salespeople to aid them in obtaining subscriptions.

subscription salesperson One who solicits subscriptions for publications. The person may receive compensation on either salary or commission basis, or both.

total city plan Plan used by some newspapers for reporting their city zone or primary market area circulation in totals instead of analyzing it under various headings such as "carriers" and "single-copy sales." Also called "metropolitan plan."

total paid Total of all classes of a publication's distribution for which the ultimate purchasers have paid in accordance with the standards set by the rules.

unpaid copies Copies distributed either entirely free or at a price inadequate to qualify them as paid in accordance with the rules.[1]

NOTE

1. "How to Read a Newspaper Audit Report," March 1984, Audit Bureau of Circulations, Schaumburg, Illinois.

Index

ABOUT THE AUTHOR ————————

W. Parkman Rankin, Ph.D., is Professor, Walter Cronkite School of Journalism and Telecommunication at Arizona State University. Prior to joining academe in January 1982, he held executive positions at *Newsweek* magazine, Time Inc., *This Week* magazine, *Redbook* magazine, and the Gannett Corporation. In addition to his teaching position he is also a consultant to *The Arizona Republic* and *The Phoenix Gazette* in Phoenix, Arizona.

Dr. Rankin has written *Selling Retail Advertising*, *The Technique of Selling Magazine Advertising*, and *Business Management of General Consumer Magazines*, 1st and 2nd editions. Dr. Rankin holds a B.S. from the Newhouse School of Public Communication at Syracuse University, and a M.B.A. and Ph.D. from New York University. He is a member of Delta Pi Epsilon Business Education Honorary Fraternity, Sigma Delta Chi, and Alpha Delta Sigma. He is also a member of the New York Dutch Treat Club and the New York Metropolitan Advertising Golf Association. He is married to the former Ruth E. Gerard and lives in Tempe, Arizona and Bomoseen, Vermont.

The Rankins have two children, Mrs. Joan Rankin Stankus, a school teacher, and Douglas W. Rankin, advertising director of the Lafayette, Indiana *Journal & Courier*.